AGENDA

CASEBOOK

CASEBOOK

DAVID COTTON AND ROGER OWEN

Lecturers in English as a Foreign Language
at the City of London Polytechnic

Harrap London

First published in Great Britain 1980
by HARRAP LIMITED
19–23 Ludgate Hill, London EC4M 7PD

Reprinted: 1981 (*twice*); 1982

ISBN 0 245–53346–X

Illustrations by
Ray Fishwick

Design and cover by
Bernard Crossland Associates

NOTE
All the places, characters and incidents in
this book are entirely fictitious and bear no
relation whatsoever to any known person,
firm or company.

ACKNOWLEDGMENTS

We should like to thank the following for
permission to reproduce photographs: courtesy
A.E.C. Electric Fencing Ltd (p. 34); Camera Press
(p. 77); Keystone Press Agency (pp. 57, 72);
courtesy Park Plaza Hotel, Toronto (p. 74); courtesy
Philips Electrical Ltd (p. 109); Popperfoto (pp. 55, 78).
We should also like to thank A.E.C. Electric
Fencing Ltd for their help and cooperation.

Dépôt légal pour cette édition: juin 1982

Printed in England by J. W. Arrowsmith Ltd, Bristol.

AGENDA is a collection of twenty separate cases, specially written for business and management students. It is suitable for the native speaker and for the student whose mother tongue is not English. It can be used with students whose English is of intermediate standard (near Cambridge First Certificate, for example) and with more advanced students (Cambridge Proficiency).

The case studies are intended to develop the communication skills which today's executive must command. The students are required to discuss a range of possible solutions to the problems presented and to decide which one should be finally recommended.

The accompanying Workbook contains a full programme of related language practice work and written assignments. Recorded cassettes or tapes are available which contain the Workbook dialogues and extra practice material. The Teacher's Book contains notes and suggestions to help the teacher in exploiting the Casebook and Workbook material and also gives the key to the Workbook exercises.

AGENDA has been developed during six years of specialist English teaching with students from all over the world. Its twenty case studies are the result of intensive classroom experience and testing.

CONTENTS

HOW TO USE THIS BOOK

THE THREE-STAGE APPROACH

Each case study can be tackled in several ways, depending on the level of the students, the instructor's assessment of their needs, and the time available. The simplest approach is in three stages:

1 Read the text of the case and the courses of action that are suggested.

2 Unless the student group is very small in number, divide it into sub-groups of three or four members each. These sub-groups should conduct a preliminary survey of the problem, the issues involved, and the implications of each of the proposed solutions.

Alternatively, each sub-group (or each student, in a small group) can study a section of the information and present it during the final discussion phase (stage 3).

3 Get the whole group back together and appoint a chairman. The group will then discuss the problem and decide what course of action should be adopted. Guidance on 'How to chair a meeting' will be found on page 11. The group may eventually agree on one of the courses of action suggested, reject them all in favour of a new proposal, or work out a compromise solution. There is not intended to be any 'right' answer to any of the problems in this book. All that matters is that a decision must be made, acceptable to everyone in the group, within a reasonable time.

HOW LONG DOES IT TAKE?

A case study needs at least $1\frac{1}{2}$ to 2 hours of class time if it is to be properly exploited. Intermediate students will probably want to study the text in some detail, with help from the teacher. Those with advanced English will get through the text more quickly and may prefer to study it in their own time before the class meets. About 15 minutes will then be sufficient to clear up any points of idiom or usage, and the rest of the time can be devoted to discussion of the problem.

ELABORATING THE THREE-STAGE APPROACH

1 Vocabulary, idiom, style, register

The texts range widely across formal and informal English, the technical language and slang of various aspects of business, and the language of different media and situations. Students may find it useful to discuss the meanings of words and phrases, or the characteristics of styles and registers, provided they are not encouraged to go too far outside the limits of their language ability when they are actively using English.

2 Dialogues

These can also be used for dialogue-reading practice.

3 Problem analysis

Many students, if they do not have a very extensive background in business studies, find it hard to appreciate fully what *kind* of problem they are dealing with in a particular case, or what subsidiary problems or questions underlie it. A few minutes spent on problem analysis may therefore be useful for the subsequent discussion period. Notes to guide the teacher for each case will be found in the Teacher's Book.

4 Reaching a decision

The type of business meeting people most often find themselves attending is an informal or semi-formal discussion; decisions at such meetings are usually made on the basis of common agreement, not on a formal vote. We suggest that chairmen of these case-study meetings should be discouraged from putting motions and counting hands, unless a consensus appears to be quite impossible to reach within the given time; in this case, a vote must be taken, but only as a last resort.

5 Role-playing

Few instructions are given in this book for role-playing; the students, in discussions of the problem, usually remain themselves. The instructor may, however, designate sub-groups to speak in favour of the different options at the final meeting, to ensure that each case is fairly put, or may turn the final discussion into a full role-playing activity.

6 The teacher's part in the final meeting

This is entirely up to the teacher to decide; he or she may join in, lead the debate, intervene occasionally, or simply observe.

7 Written assignments and follow-ups

A full programme of related language practice and written work will be found in the Workbook (see below).

To sum up, each case study can follow these stages:

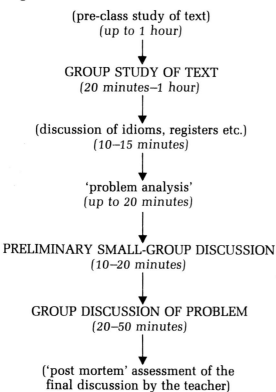

(pre-class study of text)
(up to 1 hour)

GROUP STUDY OF TEXT
(20 minutes–1 hour)

(discussion of idioms, registers etc.)
(10–15 minutes)

'problem analysis'
(up to 20 minutes)

PRELIMINARY SMALL-GROUP DISCUSSION
(10–20 minutes)

GROUP DISCUSSION OF PROBLEM
(20–50 minutes)

('post mortem' assessment of the final discussion by the teacher)
(up to 15 minutes)

THE WORKBOOK AND CASSETTES

A detailed programme of language work, closely linked with the case studies, is provided in the Workbook. Each case study has its accompanying Workbook unit, the contents of a typical unit being as follows:

- questions to aid full comprehension of the case and 'problem analysis';
- a vocabulary exercise to help the student to become familiar with specialist terms relevant to that particular case study;
- a dialogue based on various means of expressing a given idea, notion or concept (for example, 'urgency', 'permission'), together with a role-play exercise based on these means of expression;
- a numeracy exercise in which students have to express non-linguistic concepts – of number, spatial relationship and so on – in English;
- a written 'register transfer' exercise, in which the student is asked to re-write, for example, a brief informal conversation in the formal language of a business letter, or to write down what he would say if he had to explain, in a telephone conversation with a friend, the terms of a formal agreement;
- written assignments (business letters and memos, reports, cables and telex messages), with detailed suggestions to help the student carry them out successfully;
- a number of colloquial expressions which the foreign speaker is likely to hear used in business contexts and which may puzzle him if he has not been introduced to them.

A short Appendix to the Workbook contains examples of the main types of business document which also appear in the written assignments – letter, memo, report, and telex.

Recorded cassettes or tapes are also available for use with the Workbook. They contain the Workbook dialogues and other language practice material.

The Teacher's Book contains notes for the teacher on how to use the Casebook and the Workbook, and the key to some Workbook exercises.

HOW TO CHAIR A MEETING

There are no rules for being a chairman; these are only suggestions. A good chairman should be firm but not aggressive. He or she should guide the discussion but not dominate it. Although he may occasionally have to say quite a lot, he will usually say as little as possible.

1 Get people's attention and start the meeting

Right.	Let's start,		everybody?
	Let's get down to business,	shall we,	
Now then.	Can we get started,		ladies and gentlemen?
	Can I have your attention, please,		

2 Announce the business of the meeting

The	big	question	we've got to	tackle	concerns...	
			I'd like to	consider		production schedules.
	major	problem	I think we ought to	discuss	is	what Blik are going to do about . . .
				talk about		whether Bonhomme should . . .

3 Remind the group of the most important facts

As you know,		Hi-Flite has been getting complaints . . .	
I think most people know that			
The	point	is that	Westmeath is facing the possibility
	problem		of massive redundancies . . .

You may find that people want to start giving their views before you have even finished introducing the topic. In that case, go straight on to Tables 5 and 6 below. On the other hand, you may find that everyone is reluctant to speak first. You then have to make them talk.

4 Ask for people's views

	would you like to say something about this?
John,	I think you know something about this problem.
	what are your views on this?
	do you have any ideas about this one?
Perhaps you'd like to comment, Suzanne.	

If John and Suzanne don't have much to say, keep on going round the table – somebody will say something controversial before long. Chairmen of these case-study meetings, by the way, should try to make sure that every member of the group says something and contributes to the discussion.

5 Keep the discussion relevant

	Let's not I don't think we ought to	talk about get onto	exporting	just yet. at this stage.

Hold on!
Just a minute!

Can we Perhaps we could	come back to that point in a moment?
We'll	come back to be coming back to	arrangements for staff training later.
Don't let's	lose sight of the main point. get sidetracked.

6 Keep the discussion orderly

What happens if you find yourself in charge of a group which is noisy, abusive, or bad-tempered?

Just a moment, Pierre; can I come to you when Ali's finished?

We can't all speak at once. John first; then Mary; then Hari.

Quiet, please! I must ask you to treat this matter seriously.

I'm sorry, Claudia; would you mind addressing your remarks to the chair?

I don't think we need	bring personalities into this. get personal about this, do we?

We seem to be arguing at cross purposes.

Could we get back onto common ground for a moment?

7 Lead the discussion towards a conclusion

A common fault among inexperienced chairmen is to let the discussion wander on aimlessly towards no particular conclusion. Give your group plenty of chance to say all that they have to say, but remember that they have got to agree on a decision — and they should feel, at the end, that they really have agreed, not that the chairman bullied or tricked them into accepting something they didn't really want.

Well now:	does anyone else wish	to say anything? to make any further points?
	any further comments?	

Right:	I'm afraid we must bring this discussion to a close. now everyone's had their say. I think we've covered everything.

8 Confirm that there is general agreement

Are we all	agreed on in favour of	this? this proposal?

Can I take it that everyone is happy with this?

It seems	we're agreed we all agree	that Tanskin should . . .

Well, it looks as if we're broadly in agreement on this.

9 Close the meeting

Right:	that's all that's the lot I think we can call it a day;	for today;	thank you,	everyone. ladies and gentlemen.

CASE STUDIES

BONHOMME

A French company, Bonhomme, has been taken over by the Brant Corporation, a US multinational. Soon afterwards, Brant's President faces senior Bonhomme executives in what is meant to be a reassuring 'getting to know you' session.

HOW IT ALL STARTED

About thirty senior executives were waiting in a large conference room at Bonhomme's headquarters in Paris. Some were talking loudly, others cracking jokes, in an obvious attempt to appear relaxed. A thick layer of tobacco smoke hung over the room.

At last, the President of Brant arrived. The silence was instant.

'Good afternoon, ladies and gentlemen,' he said. 'I have asked your President, Mr Duperrier, to let me introduce myself. My name, as you may already know, is Carlson J. Overend Junior. I'm the President of Brant Corporation.' One or two people in the room exchanged rapid whispers.

'I set up this meeting with you today because I wanted to tell you personally how our takeover of Bonhomme is going to affect you all. Sure, we're going to make changes – shake up the organization chart here and there, take a hard look at personnel and products, generally try to liven things up a bit . . .' He paused. Blank faces stared at him. 'But I give you my solemn word, ladies and gentlemen, you prove your worth to us, you'll stay with the team, and the sky's the limit.'

Still no reaction from the audience. 'Strange,' he thought to himself, 'that should have made them sit up.'

Someone at the back raised his hand. 'I think, Mr Overend,' said the spokesman in careful but heavily accented English, 'that not all of us here understand you. Some of us don't speak very good English.'

Overend looked astonished: 'Are you telling me you people aren't following what I'm saying?'

The spokesman nodded his head, looked embarrassed and shrugged his shoulders.

Overend took his cigar out of his mouth and paused for a moment. Suddenly, he started jabbing it excitedly at the executives:

'You people don't know English, OK, so you're going to have to learn – FAST. You want to hold your job, you want to get on in the company, then you've got to know English.' He took a deep breath, then said to the spokesman: 'Now, you just put that into French, and make sure everyone's got the message – and I mean everyone.'

A SHAKE-UP

Bonhomme, a company based in Paris, has interests in electrical and mechanical engineering. It exports over 70 per cent of its production, some of its most profitable markets being in non-French-speaking countries.

When news of the Brant takeover was announced, a British financial journalist sent a telex back to his journal's chief industrial editor. This is what he said:

```
13864  INTMAG  LONDON
68531 PARIS

BONHOMME  TAKEN  OVER  BY  US  MULTINATIONAL  BRANT.   NOW  WHOLLY
OWNED  BRANT  SUBSIDIARY.    DEAL  GIVES  BONHOMME  GREATER
CAPITAL  BACKING  ALSO  ACCESS  TO  BRANT  TECHNICAL  KNOW-HOW.
BONHOMME  NOW  ABLE  TO  TENDER  FOR  MAJOR  PROJECTS  ON  MORE
COMPETITIVE  TERMS.    BUT  MAY  LOSE  HAPPY  FAMILY  ATMOSPHERE.
BRANT  LIKELY  TO  SHAKE  UP  BONHOMME  ORGANIZATION,  PERSONNEL
AND  PRODUCTS.
```

One of these shake-ups occurred shortly after the meeting with Overend.

Bonhomme's Personnel Manager, Jean Pinot, was summoned to the office of M. Duperrier, the Bonhomme President. He told Pinot that Brant's President had not been joking. Overend wanted an English language training programme put into effect without delay. Pinot was instructed to drop all but the most pressing work and to produce a report defining which groups in the company needed English language training and how urgent that need was.

'Ask around, contact anyone who can help you, even board members – we're all in the same boat,' said Duperrier, and he added with a faint smile, 'Write the report in English. I'm going to circulate it to some of the people in Brant, and I don't want them to have to translate it. They may get it wrong.'

One week later, the report 'English language proficiency in the Bonhomme company' was on Duperrier's desk. The charts below have been extracted from a section of the document. Only those personnel using English, for whatever purpose, in the normal course of their duties have been included.

1 Bonhomme personnel currently using English in the course of their duties

		GROUP	NUMBER	ENGLISH LANGUAGE PROFICIENCY *			
				FLUENT	GOOD	AVERAGE	WEAK
HEAD OFFICE (PARIS)	A	Board members	8	1	2	1	4
	B	Senior and middle management (all departments) Others of similar status	30	2	3	5	20
	C	Junior executives	27	–	5	10	12
	D	Sales staff including overseas	31	4	15	10	2
	E	Administrative staff	41	2	4	5	30
	F	Others	5	–	–	1	4
FACTORY (LILLE)	G	Senior production personnel	12	1	1	1	9
	H	Administrative staff	18	–	3	1	14
	I	Others	5	–	–	–	5
		TOTAL	177	10	33	34	100

* Personnel were asked to assess their own proficiency on a four-point scale.

2 Training needs

TRAINING	Essential and urgently needed	Essential and needed as soon as possible	Desirable when convenient
GROUP	A, B, D, G	C, E, H	F, I
Numbers who are weak or average in these categories	52	72	10

Once the report had been circulated, Jean Pinot started investigating ways of setting up a language training scheme. While doing this, he got a surprise call from Overend who was still in Paris and had received a copy of the report. Brant's President made two points, which he later confirmed in a memo to Pinot. These are reproduced below:

```
1 Brant will finance the training scheme
for one year. Results will then be re-
viewed. Any programme proposed by Pinot
will be rigorously scrutinized for cost
effectiveness.

2 Promising junior executives may well be
promoted to important positions in Brant
Corporation at some future date.
```

After a number of telephone calls, letters and discussions with organizations and individuals involved in English language training, Pinot decided that he would present for consideration four possible approaches to the problem. These are outlined below:

THE FOUR OPTIONS

1 Bonhomme could use the services of the New Horizon Study Center, an independent language school whose premises are about two kilometres from Bonhomme's offices. Established two years ago, the school is run by an American who has constantly been sending publicity material to Jean Pinot. It runs specialist English courses for professional groups, and also general English courses. The Director has offered tailor-made, full- or part-time courses for Bonhomme staff at his school. These courses will be fairly expensive. The school at present has no language laboratory.

2 The English Language Training Adviser from the Paris office of the British International Advisory Council has a different approach to the problem. He believes that since Brant considers English language training to be a top priority, Bonhomme should do things properly and send staff on short, intensive courses to an English-speaking country – preferably Britain. He would offer advice on suitable courses and provide a number of contacts.

3 A representative of a Swedish company has made an interesting offer. His company sells ultra-modern language laboratories and complete audio-visual courses for self-tuition. He argues that Bonhomme are going to need these one day, so the company might as well invest in them now. He claims the courses have been successful in other European countries. The sophisticated package he offers, which includes the installation of a language laboratory, is expensive, but seems good value for money.

4 Pinot himself feels that the company could start in a modest fashion by appointing a full-time English language instructor/administrator. This person would be empowered to hire other part-time teachers as and when necessary. The courses would be given on the company's premises, although there might be a few problems finding suitable rooms, and they would be developed slowly and steadily. Personnel urgently needing training would be given priority on the courses that were set up.

INSTRUCTIONS

First, divide into small groups of three or four, and discuss, in general terms, the type of English language training most suitable for a company like Bonhomme. Then consider each option in turn, and weigh up the advantages and disadvantages. Each group should then decide which programme or programmes Bonhomme should adopt.

Everyone should finally meet in one large group under the guidance of a chairman. A decision must now be reached on an appropriate language training programme for the company.

CHAIRS

About a month ago, in a small English university, a joint staff/student planning committee met to discuss what kind of furniture should be purchased for the Students' Common Room in a new Arts faculty block. The meeting was chaired by the university's Chief Purchasing Officer. Here are some of the comments made by staff and student representatives:

LET'S BEAR IN MIND THAT THE PEAK PERIODS WILL BE ELEVEN TO ELEVEN-THIRTY IN THE MORNING AND THREE TO THREE-THIRTY IN THE AFTERNOON. AT THOSE TIMES, AS MANY AS A HUNDRED AND FIFTY PEOPLE COULD BE USING THE COMMON ROOM. MOST OF THEM WILL BE SITTING DOWN DRINKING COFFEE OR TEA.

I AGREE WE SHOULDN'T THROW MONEY AWAY. TAKE THE PANORAMIC WINDOWS IN THE COMMON ROOM. THEY GIVE A MARVELLOUS VIEW OF THE PARK, BUT THE PLANS FOR THOSE WERE DRAWN UP WHEN WE HAD PLENTY OF MONEY.

YES, WE MUST BE ABLE TO RELAX THERE, BUT IT WILL ALSO BE A PLACE WHERE WE EXCHANGE IDEAS WITH EACH OTHER AND WITH LECTURERS. ACTUALLY, OUTSIDE THE COFFEE BREAKS, SEMINARS WILL, IN FACT, BE HELD THERE FROM TIME TO TIME.

BACKGROUND INFORMATION

Dudley Morris is the Chief Purchasing Officer of this recently established university, located about forty miles south of London. He took over the job about six years ago, and at first life was easy for him. Recently, however, things have changed. Cuts in government expenditure have drastically reduced the money available for furniture and equipment; at the same time, inflation has pushed prices up. Instead of being left to administer his funds as he sees fit, Dudley now finds himself attending meeting after meeting as every penny of expenditure is carefully scrutinized by staff, students and managers.

His principal anxiety at the moment is the new Arts block, which is to be opened by a member of the Royal Family in six weeks' time. Preparations for the event have been exhausting; there has been a tremendous row, for example, over the carpets for the new Students' Common Room. This room has a polished woodblock floor, and several thousand pounds have been spent on a number of large rugs to cover the central area of the room. Dudley had never realized how many ways there are to cover the floor of a large room until he heard them all argued over in detail by his cost-conscious colleagues. That nightmare seems to be over, but another has begun. A day or two ago he received a telephone call from the university's Finance Officer.

The Finance Officer did not beat about the bush. 'I know this is going to upset your plans, Dudley, but I'm afraid we won't be able to let you have twelve thousand pounds for the purchase of Common Room chairs after all. Things are really tight financially. You'll have to make do with six . . . Yes, that's right – I did say six thousand! . . . Now, take it easy . . . Yes, I know you've been working awfully hard. I'm sorry, but you'll just have to contact some other suppliers and see what you can come up with. You'd better get moving. We've got another committee meeting in a week's time, and we want to settle the matter of the chairs then.'

OFFERS RECEIVED FROM FURNITURE SUPPLIERS

It is the night before the committee meeting. Dudley has just finished summarizing the information gained from certain furniture companies. Copies will be distributed at the beginning of the meeting. Here are the offers which will be considered by the committee members.

1 Supplier: Universal Furniture & Fittings Ltd (UFF)

Designation: Club armchairs and sofas

Manufacturer: A well-known British company

Quantity: 60 (50 armchairs, 10 sofas seating 3 persons)

Description: Originally the property of a smart London club, the goods were acquired by UFF at a liquidation sale.

The chairs and sofas are beautifully made, luxurious and comfortable. They are covered with black leather. Although 'used' in appearance, they are far from shabby. The supplier claims they will last a lifetime.

Price:	Armchairs	£80
	Sofas	£140

The armchairs are bulky (1.2 metres in breadth). They are heavy and difficult to move. The sofas are just over 3 metres in length.

Delivery: See special conditions

This kind of furniture was made in 'the good old days'. The styling and quality belong to a bygone era.

Special conditions: The supplier will not split up the goods. These are offered on an 'all or nothing' basis. Also, the buyer must pay transport costs from UFF warehouse to the university – a distance of approximately 50 kilometres.

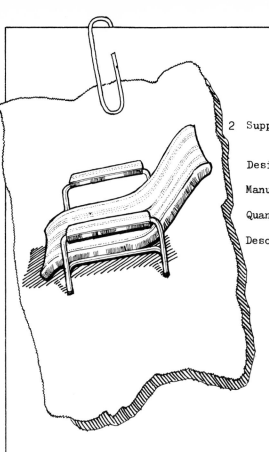

2 Supplier: Godfrey & Son Ltd

Designation: 'Sit-U-Rite' semi-reclining chairs

Manufacturer: Andersson Furniture Co., Denmark

Quantity: No limitation

Description: Very modern design, fairly
comfortable to sit in. Made
out of glass-reinforced
plastic with foam padding
and nylon covers. Metal
frames.

Colours: bright red, yellow,
pale blue.

Difficult to assess durability
— three to five years, perhaps,
with normal use.

Although relaxing to sit in,
the chairs are not ideal for
coffee-drinkers. Also, the
feet will possibly scratch and
mark wooden floors. The chairs
are light and very easy to move.

Price: £45 each. For purchases
in excess of 50, the unit
price is reduced to £40.

Delivery: 4 to 6 weeks following receipt of an order. Prices
include free delivery.

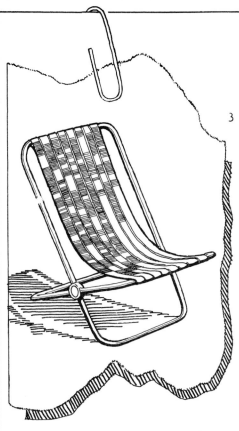

3 Supplier: WSF Ltd (Scotland)

Designation: 'Baugruppe' folding chairs

Manufacturer: A Japanese company based in
West Germany

Quantity: No limitation

Description: These folding chairs have
chromed tubular frames.
Their backs and seats are
woven from strips of 14-oz
denim. They are a mass-
produced, standardized line
of this Japanese company.

Colours: white, red and green.

The chairs are as comfortable
as can be expected for their
price. A few felt rather
unsteady when tested, and they
have a tendency to slide on
polished floors. They also
dig into carpets a little.

Durability: a year or two with
luck. With good treatment,
even longer.

Price: £10 each. (No discounts
               for bulk purchase.)

Delivery: Two weeks from receipt of
               order. Price includes
               delivery costs.

Special conditions: This wholesale company will only accept orders
                       for 100 items or more for this particular line
                       of goods.

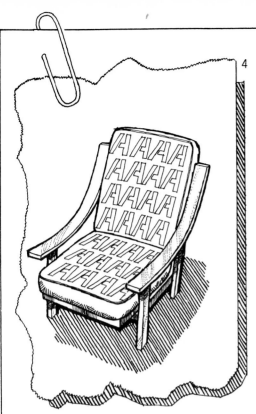

4 Supplier: City Supplies Ltd (London)

Designation: Easy chairs

Manufacturer: A British company no longer
               in business

Quantity: 120

Description: Part of a cancelled export
             order, the chairs were made
             originally by a contract
             furnishing company for an
             airport lounge in Indonesia.

             The seats, arms and backs
             are padded with foam rubber.
             They are covered in brown
             Terylene/cotton with a
             repeating design based on
             the Indonesian Airlines
             emblem. Hardwood frames.

             Comfortable, ideal for re-
             laxing in.

             Durability: with normal
             student use, possibly three
             years or more.

Price: £4,800. (Goods sold as
                one lot.)

Special conditions: Buyer collects. Distance from supplier to
                        university approximately 70 kilometres.

INSTRUCTIONS

Meet first in small groups of three or four people. These should discuss the following questions:
- What is a Students' Common Room used for?
- What characteristics do you look for in furniture which is to be used in public places?
- Should the size and shape of the room influence the choice of furniture? The Common Room is L–shaped, and has a floor area of just under 220 square metres.

Each small group should decide which chairs it considers most suitable.

Then, meeting in one large group with a chairman, students should make a final decision as to how the budget of £6,000 should be spent.

MARKETING PERSONNEL SERVICES
CLIENT RECORD CARD

E

COMPANY NAME   Elite Footwear Co. Ltd
ADDRESS   Blackthorn Mills, Kendal, Cumbria, England
TELEPHONE   Kendal 472159   TELEX   25015015
PRODUCT   Luxury-grade shoes (hand-crafted leather – bison, antelope, crocodile, suede, etc.)
INITIAL ENQUIRY   Received 15 December 1979
DATA   Marketing strategy concentrated on carefully chosen objectives.
Since 1975 Elite have operated through Far East Footwear Corporation, selling principally to big importers, mail order firms and department stores.

Sales: (US $)		1979	1980 (anticipated)
			1.25m
	Japan	1m	up to 1m
	Hong Kong	0.5m	

Current contract with Far East Footwear expires July 1980 and will not be renewed (by mutual agreement).

REQUIREMENTS/VACANCIES
Client wishes to   (i) increase sales through existing channels
                  (ii) develop integrated marketing strategy in the Far East
                  (iii) prepare market for introduction of new products – company plans to diversify into giftware, travel goods, clothing.
May set up subsidiary sales company.
                  (iv) penetrate Singapore market.

Require Sales Representative – no special requirements, but must have good background in retail selling. Salary range $18 – 22,000
ACTION   Post advertised in English-language press, January 1980.
Interviews, Tokyo, 13 – 15 February 1980.
Elite notified of recommendations, 19 February.

79/7501   ELITE FOOTWEAR CO.LTD   Sales Representative

MPS TAKE ACTION

Nigel Thompson, Managing Director of Elite Footwear, receives a telephone call from Toshi Kazumichi, the head of Marketing Personnel Services.

Thompson Hullo – Mr Kazumichi? Thompson speaking.

Kazumichi Hullo, Mr Thompson! Concerning the appointment of a Far East Sales Representative for your company: I'm glad to say that we had a good response to our advertisement. We have a number of applications which look very promising.

Thompson Well, that's good news. Have you selected any of them?

Kazumichi We have shortlisted four. I'd like you to see their particulars and give us your opinion before we finally make the appointment on your behalf.

Thompson I don't mind commenting, but it's a bit tricky, with nothing but the application forms to go on.

Kazumichi We've investigated each of these people in some depth, Mr Thompson; I think you'll find the data is pretty comprehensive. I'll put all the stuff in the post tonight, unless you would like it telexed?

Thompson No, no, airmail will do.

Kazumichi You should get it by the end of the week. Goodbye for now, Mr Thompson.

Thompson Goodbye, Mr Kazumichi – thanks for calling.

THE FOUR CANDIDATES

Towards the end of the same week, Thompson receives photostats of four cards from MPS's confidential files.

NAME John CHUNG   **NATIONALITY** British (Hong Kong)

DOMICILE Kowloon, H.K.   **AGE** 29

MARITAL STATUS Divorced – supports 2 children who live with their mother.

PRESENT EMPLOYER Far East Footwear Corp.

SINCE April 1975

POSITION Sales representative. Sells imported shoes etc. to Japanese and Hong Kong importers, department stores and mail order houses.

REASON FOR LEAVING Dissatisfied; says salary does not reflect his contribution to company profits.

PREVIOUS EXPERIENCE Mail order clerk; shop assistant in retail shoe store.

EDUCATION Completed secondary school. Currently attends evening classes at local polytechnic – hopes to obtain Diploma in Marketing.

LANGUAGES Fluent Cantonese; excellent English; good Japanese.

SALES ABILITY TEST 88%   **IQ SCORE** 116

PERSONALITY Appeared energetic, confident, likeable, articulate. Impressive knowledge of Hong Kong and Japanese markets; had obviously read up on Singapore market. Tall, slim. Expensive, flashy suit.

FURTHER INFORMATION Highly thought of in present firm (though it was suggested he works in bursts – very hard for a period, then relaxes). Said to be sometimes in debt; lives above his income. Gregarious, likes night life, parties.

SALARY EXPECTED US $15,000 with car and gasoline allowance.

NAME John PEARWICK **NATIONALITY** British

DOMICILE Nagoya, Japan **AGE** 50

MARITAL STATUS Single

PRESENT EMPLOYER For the last 15 years Mr Pearwick
SINCE has run his own business importing leather goods,
POSITION costume jewellery and giftware from Europe.

REASON FOR LEAVING He no longer wants the responsibility
of managing a profitable but time-consuming business.

PREVIOUS EXPERIENCE Salesman for motor manufacturer; manager of large UK car-hire
organization; short period farming; diplomatic service (British Embassy,Tokyo '63-5).

EDUCATION English public school; M.A. (London) in Political Economy; post-graduate
course : Diploma in Business Administration.

LANGUAGES Exceptional; languages are his principal hobby. Virtually bilingual English/Japanese; good spoken/written Mandarin; acquainted with other oriental languages.

SALES ABILITY TEST 73% **IQ SCORE** 140

PERSONALITY Highly intelligent, cultured, very sophisticated. Not an extrovert —
rather intense manner. Listened intently to questions, gave very precise answers.
Small man, but with great presence. Soberly and immaculately dressed.

FURTHER INFORMATION Lives with friend (male) in luxury high-rise apartment.
Financially secure; could retire now if he wished. Good contacts with Japanese
government officials, intimate knowledge of Japanese and Far Eastern markets. Had a
breakdown 8 years ago, but claims to be in excellent health now.

SALARY EXPECTED US $25,000 plus car and expenses; bonus scheme based on sales results.

NAME Anita KATO **NATIONALITY** Japanese
(mother British)

DOMICILE Kyoto, Japan **AGE** 34

MARITAL STATUS Married, with one child, age 6

PRESENT EMPLOYER Japanese Footwear Importing Co.
SINCE 1978 (Spring)
POSITION Chief shoe buyer (responsible for purchasing shoes from
10 countries for domestic market).
REASON FOR LEAVING Desires more variety, possibility of travel.
Attracted by 'the challenge of selling'.

PREVIOUS EXPERIENCE Filing clerk; sales assistant (one year); book-keeper;
assistant buyer (with Japanese Footwear).

EDUCATION Did not finish secondary school. 5 years' evening classes — secretarial
subjects, book-keeping. Recently completed correspondence course:export marketing.

LANGUAGES Fluent Japanese and English. Some Mandarin.

SALES ABILITY TEST 78% **IQ SCORE** 125

PERSONALITY A human dynamo — great energy, vivacious, enthusiastic, extrovert.
Smiled a lot. Claimed to be very competitive — said she didn't like to lose,
especially at bridge and mahjong. Medium height, slim, well dressed.

FURTHER INFORMATION According to a colleague, Mrs Kato 'shot to the top like a
rocket' in her present firm. Well liked, in spite of success. Loves children:talks
of adopting a second child. Marriage rumoured to be on the verge of breaking up.

SALARY EXPECTED US $18,000 with company car.

NAME Paolo J.-M. RIZAL   **NATIONALITY** Singaporean
(born in Manila)

DOMICILE Singapore   **AGE** 38

MARITAL STATUS Married, with 5 children

PRESENT EMPLOYER Choi Shoe Manufacturing Corp.
SINCE Late 1977
POSITION Sales representative covering Singapore and
Malaysia, selling to wholesale and retail shoe outlets.
REASON FOR LEAVING Claims firm expected him to work
18 hours a day.
PREVIOUS EXPERIENCE Salesman for a number of Singapore-based distributors,
mainly in clothing/footwear.
EDUCATION Did exceptionally well at secondary school, but dropped out of university.
Later obtained Diploma in Marketing: 1-year course at well-known business college.
LANGUAGES Good English; fluent Spanish and Tagalog; good spoken and fair written
Cantonese; some Japanese.
SALES ABILITY TEST 80%   **IQ SCORE** 120

PERSONALITY Totally relaxed, self-assured, friendly; talked sensibly about Far East
market potential, but not afraid to discuss subjects of general interest. Tall,
intellectual-looking, short hair; clothes simple but elegant and fashionable.
FURTHER INFORMATION Happily married to pretty Malaysian wife who likes entertaining
and is expert cook. Brother in Hong Kong owns chain of general stores:dress materials, clothing, giftware etc. Appears to enjoy being thought a bit of a character;
full of ideas - some rather far-fetched. Apparently liked by his colleagues, but it
was suggested by former employer that he lacked drive.
SALARY EXPECTED   US $20,000 with all expenses.

INSTRUCTIONS

Meet first of all in small groups of three or four students. Each group should discuss the following:

- What qualifications or characteristics would make an applicant ideal for this post?
- How does each of the four people on the shortlist match up to your specification?
- Which applicant should Mr Thompson choose as the Sales Representative in the Far East?

The whole group should then come together for their final discussion, at the end of which they must decide who is to get the job.

FUNFABBRIX FASHIONS

FIRE EXIT

OFFICE

NO ENTRY

STRICTLY NO SMOKING

ON THE TOP FLOOR OF A RICKETY OLD BUILDING IN THE EAST END OF LONDON, FUNFABBRIX FASHIONS MAKES SMART CLOTHES TO BE SOLD IN THE BOUTIQUES AND DEPARTMENT STORES OF THE WEST END.

ALMOST ALL THE WORKERS ARE WOMEN, MOST OF THEM IMMIGRANTS.

THE WORKSHOP IS A CROWDED, NOISY, CONFUSED, UNCOMFORTABLE BUT CHEERFUL PLACE. THE SEWING MACHINES HUM AND THE RACKS OF DRESSES KEEP ROLLING OUT.

EVERYONE WORKS HOURS AND HOURS OF OVERTIME EVERY WEEK BECAUSE THEY NEED THE MONEY.

FURS AND SKINS

FUNFABBRIX

WHOLE SALE ONLY

VACANCIES
CUTTERS
PRESSERS

FUNF FASHIONS

BENNO STARTED LIFE BY WORKING ON HIS PARENTS' FRUIT AND VEGETABLE STALL. SOMEHOW, HE FOUND HIMSELF WORKING FOR FUNFABBRIX, IN THE CRAMPED LITTLE 'OFFICE' IN ONE CORNER OF THE WORKSHOP.

BENNO MACARI (AGED 22) IS THE PRODUCTION MANAGER.

EVERY FRIDAY AFTERNOON, THE BOSS DRIVES UP IN HIS ROLLS-ROYCE AND PAYS BENNO HIS 'SALARY' IN USED £5 NOTES. THIS CAN GO ON FOR YEARS - PROVIDED BENNO NEVER GIVES HIM A MOMENT'S ANXIETY!

BENNO'S OWN ANXIETIES ARE CENTRED ON THE SUPERVISOR OF HIS WORKSHOP - **MRS EDNA WHITESON**.

MRS WHITESON LOVES ALL 'HER GIRLS' AND IS CONSTANTLY DEMANDING BETTER WORKING CONDITIONS FOR THEM.

NO ONE IN THE SHOP BELONGS TO A TRADE UNION, BUT MRS WHITESON CAN ORGANIZE VERY EFFECTIVE INDUSTRIAL ACTION ON HER OWN.

SHE IS ESPECIALLY WORRIED THAT THE WORKSHOP CONTRAVENES THE LAW RELATING TO HEALTH AND SAFETY AT WORK. FOR INSTANCE, NOT LONG AGO A SIMILAR CLOTHING WORKSHOP IN THE NEXT STREET WAS TOTALLY DESTROYED BY FIRE. SEVERAL PEOPLE WERE INJURED.

THREE MONTHS AGO, THE LOCAL GOVERNMENT FIRE INSPECTOR VISITED FUNFABBRIX FASHIONS...

THIS FIRE EXTINGUISHER HASN'T BEEN CHECKED OR TESTED FOR NEARLY THREE YEARS!

NOT MUCH PRESSURE IN THIS HOSE, IS THERE?

BREWING TEA ON A GAS RING IN A CONFINED SPACE CAN BE A MAJOR FIRE HAZARD!

ALL THIS OLD PAINT WOULD BURN LIKE A TORCH!

—AND THESE BOXES ARE BLOCKING THE EMERGENCY EXIT—GET THEM MOVED!

AS HE WALKS HOME THROUGH THE RAIN, BENNO MACARI REVIEWS THE COURSES OF ACTION OPEN TO HIM.

WHAT SHOULD BENNO MACARI DO?

THE LEGAL POSITION

Funfabbrix is a problem of human relations, not law. But when you discuss it you will need to know a little about the law of employment as it stood in England at the time of this story – in 1978. This area of the law is extremely complex, but two Acts of Parliament, or Statutes, have attempted to make it a little simpler.

The Health and Safety at Work Act 1974 made every employee responsible, in principle, for his own safety and that of other workers around him. Supervisors (such as Mrs Whiteson) and safety representatives now play a big part in making workplaces safer. In every organization, one manager is made responsible for the observance of safety regulations. Every employer must publish, and observe, a written statement of the firm's health and safety policy. Factory inspectors can issue 'improvement notices' if they think premises are dangerous; this, in effect, is what the inspector in the Funfabbrix case does. The employer can appeal against the improvement notice if he feels it is unreasonable, but if he does not he has 21 days in which to improve safety conditions on his premises. However, there are about 250,000 workplaces in England and Wales, and only 600 inspectors to visit them all; many smaller premises, and some larger ones, therefore evade many of the provisions of the law.

The Employment Protection Act 1975 made an employee's job in effect his personal property, not to be taken from him without very good reason. All dismissals are presumed to be unfair, and to deserve payment of compensation, unless the employer can satisfy the court that dismissal was justified. However, dismissal – with or without notice – is recognised to be justified in many situations, e.g. an employee's refusal to obey a 'lawful and reasonable' order, or refusal to work overtime if overtime is compulsory, or customary, and the employee knew this when he took the job. There is a contract between employer and employee, and a breach of this, by either side, may lead to legal action. But Edna Whiteson's position is much stronger than Macari's or that of Funfabbrix Fashions. Refusal to work overtime because employees are demanding better working conditions is usually not regarded as justifying dismissal. In any case, if Macari sacked Mrs Whiteson before the industrial action began, this would certainly be regarded as an attempt to punish her before she had broken her contract; and if he sacked her during the overtime ban, he would have to sack all the girls who were refusing to work overtime. To sack only the leader would be victimization, and Mrs Whiteson would have excellent grounds for appealing against her dismissal. Legal costs plus compensation could cost Funfabbrix several thousand pounds.

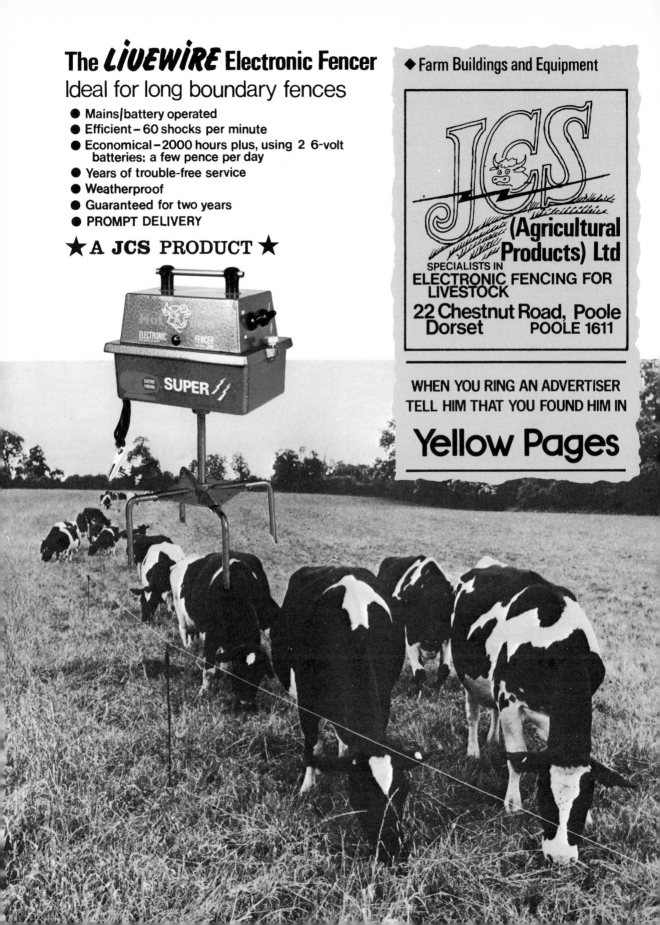

BACKGROUND

Since John Connell took over JCS Agricultural Products Ltd as Managing Director in the mid-1960s, the business has been increasingly successful.

One important reason for JCS's success is that they developed the *Livewire* electronic fencer. This is a self-contained, portable, weatherproof unit which produces a powerful shock every second. Used with electro-plastic wire, it provides an effective fence for cattle at a very low running cost. The fencer is a great advance upon earlier types because it has no moving parts and the intensity of the shock remains constant throughout the whole life of the batteries. At present, the fencer is contributing about 30 per cent of the company's profits.

Despite the success of the fencer, John Connell was totally unprepared for the problem that arose when Joe Maskie, Vice-President of Agriproducts Inc., telexed him early in December.

AN OPPORTUNITY IN CANADA FOR JCS

```
38210 JCS POOLE DORSET

58420 MASKIE AGRIPRODS EDMONTON

ATTENTION JOHN CONNELL

RE 'LIVEWIRE' FENCER

WE REQUIRE 45 UNITS SOONEST AND 20 PER MONTH FROM FEBRUARY TO END
OF YEAR.  SOME INTEREST BEING SHOWN IN YOUR ELECTRIC GATE BUT NO
FIRM ORDERS YET.

JOE MASKIE

58420 MASKIE AGRIPRODS EDMONTON

38210 JCS POOLE DORSET
```

As soon as John Connell received that telex, he put through a call to Alberta. He knew Joe to be the exciteable type, inclined to 'blow his top', as he himself often admitted. Nevertheless John was surprised by the tough attitude Joe adopted. Here is part of their conversation:

Joe Maskie You've got me over a barrel here, John. I've promised delivery of those forty-five units and I can guarantee to sell another twenty a month. Now you say you can't supply me?

John Connell I didn't say that exactly, Joe. But, be fair, you told us you would start ordering in June. I'd kind of planned for that date.

Joe Maskie Oh come on now, John. I've gone to a lot of trouble and expense to get our customers interested in your firm's products. You've got to get those fencers out to me.

John Connell Well, I'll need a little time, Joe.

Joe Maskie To hell with that. I'm not going to do business with a company that can't deliver the goods. Sure, I'll give you time. You can have a couple of days to get organized, then I want a definite answer one way or the other.

John Connell OK Joe. I'll take another look at our production capabilities and see what we can come up with.

Joe Maskie Do that, John. There are exciting prospects for you over here, but not if you can't meet the orders.

PRODUCTION OF THE *LIVEWIRE* FENCER

At present, the factory can produce a maximum of 500 electronic fencers a year. If John Connell decides to increase production beyond that amount, he will have to extend the building and invest in new machinery. To do so will involve time and money.

In 1979, sales of the fencer were as shown below:

Units	Market	(average profit per unit — %)
220	UK	(22)
60	Belgium and Holland	(26)
130	East Africa	(18)
410		

As can be seen from these figures, sales fell well below the factory's production capacity.

INFORMATION ABOUT EACH MARKET

1 The UK market

Sales of the fencer have steadily increased in the past five years but further expansion is unlikely, because of market saturation. John Connell's sales forecast for the next three years is given below:

1980	220–240 units
1981	200–220 units
1982	200 units (with a lot of luck!)

Most buyers of the electronic fencers purchase other products from the company.

2 Belgium and Holland

The company have gained a toehold in Europe by using a sole distributor, the Joachim Carpels Company, to develop sales in these two countries. This Brussels-based organization buys on its own account – not as a commission agent. It has been handling the *Livewire* fencer for two years, so far with disappointing results:

1978	40 units
1979	60 units

Sales in 1979 were in fact 50 per cent below the agreed target of 120 units. However, Joachim Carpels stressed that he had been handicapped initially by the costly tests for safety and reliability which Belgian regulations prescribed for the fencer. (He had to show, for example, that a cow would not be electrocuted if it bit through the fencing wire!) Much to John Connell's surprise, Carpels has given his personal guarantee that in 1980 his company will buy a minimum of 120 electronic fencers; indeed, he has already placed an order for 20. This organization also has subsidiaries in West Germany, Italy and France, so it offers JCS a good distribution network in the European Economic Community area.

3 The East African market

By the terms of their contract – which has one year to run – with the distributor in this area, JCS are legally bound to supply a minimum of 120 units a year unless the agent agrees in advance to take a smaller number. In the last four years, the distributor has never taken more than 150 units but never less than 120. This market has probably reached saturation point. It will slowly decline in future years.

THE PROBLEM

John Connell signed a two-year contract with Joe Maskie in late November. He was under the impression Joe would begin ordering round about June 1980. This suited him because he thought the Canadian orders would take up the probable excess capacity he would have in the factory. He reasoned that, in any case, he would be able to get rid of the Carpels agency, if necessary, because of its poor performance. Another possibility was that the British market would begin its decline in that year. The Canadian market had strongly attracted John even though average profit per unit might be as low as 15 per cent.

In the present situation, John Connell considers he has four possible courses of action:

1 Refuse to supply Joe Maskie

Legally, this is feasible, but such a decision would mean losing good sales prospects for the fencer in Canada. Also, Joe has already carried out a good deal of unpaid market research and sales promotion on behalf of the fencer and other JCS products.

2 Break off business relations with Joachim Carpels

JCS has no written contract with Carpels, simply a verbal agreement that Carpels would maintain a 'reasonable level of sales'. Dropping Carpels would mean starting from scratch to break into the EEC market. Also, there is the work Carpels has done to get the fencer tested.

3 Reduce supplies to the UK and Belgium/Holland markets

This would antagonize certain farm owners who have come to rely on JCS for fencing and other products. It would undoubtedly affect Connell's relationship with Joachim Carpels.

4 Withdraw slowly from the East African market

Put pressure on the distributor in this market to accept a substantial reduction in supplies. If necessary, threaten not to renew the contract once it expires in December. This could seriously damage JCS's prospects in African markets.

INSTRUCTIONS

First, meet in small groups and discuss the advantages and disadvantages of the four options. Finally, meet as one group under the direction of a chairman. You should then try to reach agreement on the course(s) of action JCS should take in this situation.

WATCHMERE HOSPITAL

Watchmere is part of a group of hospitals serving an industrial area. Built in the late nineteenth century, it has expanded in a piecemeal fashion, various wings and annexes being added over the years. Its present capacity is three hundred and fifty beds. There has been much talk in local government circles of building a new general hospital, but so far plans for this have not gone much beyond the blueprint stage. Given the present economic conditions, it seems likely that Watchmere will have to struggle on, underfinanced, understaffed, and lacking most of the facilities of a really modern hospital.

THE MEDICAL RECORDS DEPARTMENT

The staff of this department refer to the prefabricated building in which they work as 'the hut'. They have complained fairly regularly to their department head, Mrs Sheila Holmes, about their poor working conditions – the lack of space, poor lighting and uncomfortable office furniture. In the summer, the main office can become unpleasantly hot; in the winter, the heating system sometimes fails to heat the rooms adequately.

In this department, there are eighteen clerical staff, eight medical secretaries and three part-timers. The secretaries deal with medical records and also spend quite a lot of their time dealing with the work of the separate medical units to which they are attached. They either go over to the clinics to take dictation or the consultants come over and work with them in the main office of 'the hut'. The secretaries also operate a pool system to provide the secretarial services needed by the other medical and nursing staff in the hospital.

Mrs Holmes reports to the Hospital Secretary, Mr Jim Devenish. He in turn is responsible to the Group Secretary, Mr David Miller.

TROUBLE AMONG THE WORKERS

CONFIDENTIAL

TO Group Secretary   **FROM** Hospital Secretary

SUBJECT Medical Records Department

You will by now have received my report on the stoppage of work which occurred in the above department on 4 February. This incident reinforces my view that the department head, Mrs Sheila Holmes, lacks the managerial skills to carry out her duties effectively. You will recall that I have brought to your attention other matters leading me to question Mrs Holmes's suitability for the position she now holds.

Please let me have your thoughts on this as soon as possible.

Ref. jd/md/10   JD   7 February

David Miller, Group Secretary, groaned inwardly when he read the above memo. In the last year, Jim Devenish had been on the phone to him several times complaining about the low morale in the Medical Records Department and the poor judgement of its head, Mrs Holmes. Jim was out for her blood, no doubt about it. Nevertheless, Monday's incident had been rather serious and the problem was in fact still unresolved. He began to review in his mind the facts contained in Devenish's report.

- Monday, 4 February, was bitterly cold. The heating system in 'the hut' was apparently out of order.
- Somebody borrowed a paraffin heater from the hospital storeroom and twenty of the staff began work more or less immediately. Nine clerical workers, however, went into the staff coffee–lounge where everyone gathered round a small electric fire which was installed there. Four of these workers were Asians: two Indians, a Pakistani and a Sri Lankan.
- Mrs Holmes knew that the workers were in the lounge but did not ask them to return to work.
- The nine clerical staff remained in the rest-room from about 9 am to 10.45 am when the office was, in their view, warm enough to work in.
- Mrs Holmes did not report the incident to Jim Devenish, Hospital Secretary.
- The following day, Jim Devenish received a message that Miss Sharma Patel, one of the clerical workers, wished to speak to him about the nine 'rebel' workers. He agreed to talk to her. At their meeting, she first of all pointed out it was the hospital management's responsibility to ensure the office was adequately heated. However, the staff who had remained in the office felt that Mrs Sheila Holmes should have asked the 'rebel' workers to return to work. Her attitude had caused resentment among the other staff. Not only had they continued to work despite the cold, but it was also a particularly busy time in the Records Department. The temporary loss of nine workers added an extra burden.

A PROBLEM WITH MRS HOLMES?

After careful thought, David Miller sent this reply to Jim Devenish:

CONFIDENTIAL

TO Hospital Secretary   **FROM** Group Secretary

SUBJECT Work stoppage in Medical Records Department

This matter needs to be handled delicately. Please keep me fully informed and feel free to consult me if necessary.
Re Mrs Sheila Holmes, you appear to have completely lost confidence in her ability to do the job. I am willing to review her work record, but perhaps you could let me have in writing other evidence of her lack of judgment.

Ref. dm/pd/62   *D.M.*   8 February

On Monday, 11 February, Jim Devenish's report concerning the errors of judgment of Mrs Holmes was on the Group Secretary's desk. The most significant incidents mentioned in it are itemized below:

CONFIDENTIAL

```
REPORT ON MRS SHEILA HOLMES

1  About a year ago, Mrs Holmes met, outside office hours, the leader of the city's
Asian community.  This person told her about the high unemployment rate among Asian
immigrants, maintaining that racial prejudice was an important reason for their
difficulty in getting jobs.  Since that time, five new staff have joined the depart-
ment.  All have been of Asian origin.  In justifying her selection policy, Mrs
Holmes said to the Hospital Secretary: 'These people need a helping hand.'

2  More recently, one of the medical secretaries asked for each Friday off to at-
tend a course at the local teacher training college.  This would enable her to
qualify as a teacher of secretarial studies.  Mrs Holmes unofficially granted the
request without going through the normal channels.  This meant that the other sec-
retaries would have to work especially hard while their colleague was absent.  Mrs
Holmes's decision caused a fair amount of bad feeling in this sub-section of the
department.

3  Two months ago, after making a careful study of the department's work methods,
the Hospital Secretary decided that costs would be greatly reduced and greater
efficiency achieved if the consultants used Dictaphones for most of their corres-
pondence.  The secretaries could work from these and therefore the time they spent
going to and fro between 'the hut' and the clinics would be saved.  Mrs Holmes
accepted that the Dictaphone method would be more efficient, but refused to put it
into effect because the medical secretaries were violently opposed to it.  According
to her, the one thing they enjoyed about their job was 'the daily contacts with the
medical and nursing staff in the units.'
```

INSTRUCTIONS

First, meet in small groups and discuss these questions:

(i) Who was to blame in the heating incident?

(ii) Should the staff who refused to work lose a proportion of their pay?

(iii) Should the department head, Mrs Sheila Holmes, be retained in her present position?

(iv) Why is morale low in the Medical Records Department?

(v) What steps could be taken to improve morale in this department?

Then, join together in one large group to decide what steps should be taken to settle the present dispute and to avert problems in future.

*GALLERIA GIORDANO
Palazzo Giordano, Piazza dei
Quattro Caballi.
Open Mon-Fri 10-12, 2-5, Sat 10-1,
closed Sun & public holidays.
Admission free.

Although less well known than
it deserves, this small,
beautifully kept, somewhat
overcrowded gallery is a treasure
house for the art lover, especially
for the serious student of
seventeenth- and eighteenth-
century North Italian schools.
Founded in 1879 by the wealthy
industrialist Giacomo Campoverdi

galleria
GIORDANO
an introductory guide

**ENGLISH
EDITION**

WELCOME TO THE
GIORDANO!
In 1848, the year of the rev-
olution in Europe, a young
Italian nationalist was forced
to flee from his native town
to the United States. He
joined the California gold
rush, and made and lost a
fortune before he was
twenty-five. His second
fortune was built on firmer
foundations: iron and steel.
His name was Giacomo
Campoverdi, but he regis-
tered as a US citizen under
the name of Jimmie Green-
field, and he kept the name
even when he came back
to his native town, a millionaire, the year after Cav-
our and Garibaldi united
our Italy under King Victor
Emmanuel in 1860.
Greenfield bought the
derelict palazzo in 1879 and
set about restoring and rebuilding it. He named it after
the artist he most admired:
Luca Giordano of Naples
(1632-1705), known as
'Luca the Speedy' because
of his exceptional work-rate.
The collection of paintings
and drawings that we see
today has been greatly added to since Greenfield's
time, but his dying wish is
still faithfully observed—
that admission to the Gallery should be absolutely
free.

ITALY
Galleries in trouble
Many of Italy's prime cultural shrines
are facing severe financial problems as costs
escalate and money becomes harder to find.
Typical of these impoverished grandees is
the Giordano Gallery in Pavia, richly
endowed by Italo-American steel magnate
Jimmie Greenfield in 1879, but now facing
a bleak future. Away from major tourist
routes, and saddled with Greenfield's decree
that there must be no admission charge,
the Giordano relies on a dwindling income
from the Greenfield Foundation Trust.
Contributions from its 100,000 visitors a
year amount to a pittance, and its sale of
reproductions and publications barely
covers running costs. *Gli Amici del
Giordano*—The Friends of the Giordano—
a voluntary organization—have limited
funds and have been increasingly uneasy
about the trustees' investment policies.
Marcel Delariche, Paris representative of
the Friends commented: 'One more big
purchase, on top of the bill for structural
repairs now outstanding, will finish the
Giordano.'

42

THE TRUSTEES MEET

MINUTES of a meeting of the Trustees of the Giordano Foundation
held on Wednesday 15 April 1981
in the Salle Watteau, Institut Européen des Beaux Arts, Bruges

Present: Prof. C. van S. Huyghens (Belgium) (Chairman)
              Dr J. M. Tejero (Spain)
              Miss Maria Giulietta Campoverdi (Italy)
                (representing the Friends of the Giordano)
              V. E. M. Donatello (Italy)
              Dr J.-J. P. Lagrange (France)
              Miss E. Parkinson (Great Britain)
              F. Y. Djilovic (Yugoslavia) (Secretary)

Apologies for absence: Prof. Sangrande, Miss Eyckhardt, P. J. Smithson

1 The minutes of the previous meeting, held in Rome on 16 October 1980, were signed
and accepted.

2 The Chairman welcomed Dr Lagrange as a new member of the Board of Trustees.

3 The principal business of the meeting was to discuss the Chairman's Annual Report
and approve the allocation of funds for the coming year. Dr Lagrange at once expressed
alarm at the low level of the Foundation's resources, pointing out that the original
capital of US $5m had been eroded by inflation, short-sighted investment policies,
and the use of capital to purchase pictures. He said that the present reserve of
just over US $3m represented, in real terms, a tiny fraction of the 1879 endowment,
while the declining income from investments and publishing (about US $800,000) would
soon be insufficient to meet routine expenses.

   Dr Tejero justified the Foundation's expenditure of capital, saying that the sale
of a major work of art was always a unique opportunity. If the Gallery had relied
exclusively on its Acquisitions Fund, it would have ceased buying first-rate works
when sale-room prices escalated in the 1960s. He said that the collection itself
was worth many times what had been spent in acquiring it, and that it would be adequate
security for any bank loan.

   Sr Donatello reminded the Board that there was a credit squeeze in Italy, that
interest rates were very high, and that few banks would accept as collateral a
collection that might not, under the terms of the Founder's will, be broken up or
sold.

   Miss Parkinson thought that the Foundation would not be able to service a major
loan. She reminded the Board that she and Sr Donatello had repeatedly asked for
a working party to be set up to enquire into the Gallery's financial prospects.

BENEDETTO SCALIERI
PALAZZO GIORDANO SURVEYOR'S REPORT
MAY 1981 English translation

11 STRUCTURAL CONDITION AND DEFECTS

11.1 <u>Exterior walls</u>

In 1970 a large crack appeared in the east side of the building, and steel tie-bars were let into the stonework on the interior. Glass strips were also fixed along the line of the crack to act as telltales and indicate any further movement. These remained intact until May 1976. Since that date there has been up to 5mm of lateral displacement. The condition of the whole east wall now gives cause for alarm, although there is no question of immediate collapse. The most probable cause is subsidence,

What Scalieri didn't want to put in writing was his estimate of the cost of repairing the structural damage — AT LEAST $ 500,000 !

V.E.M.D.

AN EXCITING OPPORTUNITY

The Collector MAY 1981
A MONTHLY REVIEW OF THE INTERNATIONAL ART MARKET

SURPRISE of the month is certainly this fine canvas of 'Susannah and the Elders', discovered in a bank vault in Edinburgh and now confirmed by experts as the authentic work of Alessandro Magnasco (1677–1749). It will be auctioned by Christie's in London on 1st July and is expected to fetch upwards of £50,000.

We must have this for the Giordano! TEJERO

TIME FOR DECISIONS

SENIOR MEMBERS OF THE
BOARD OF TRUSTEES

IF THE GALLERY NEEDS MONEY, THEN WE MUST APPEAL TO THE GENEROSITY OF THE PUBLIC! LAUNCH A SAVE THE GIORDANO CAMPAIGN! IT WORKS IN BRITAIN – WHY NOT HERE?

IT'S TIME WE RECONSIDERED THE FOUNDER'S WILL. HE COULD NOT HAVE FORESEEN TWENTIETH CENTURY CONDITIONS. THE CLAUSE ABOUT PUBLIC ADMISSION WITHOUT CHARGE NEEDS TO BE RE-INTERPRETED IN THE LIGHT OF CURRENT PRACTICE. IF WE CHARGE EVEN A SMALL SUM PER PERSON (REDUCED RATES FOR STUDENTS) WE SHALL BE ABLE TO BORROW TO MEET CONTINGENCIES.

PROGRESSIVE MEMBERS
OF THE
BOARD OF TRUSTEES

THE FRIENDS OF THE GIORDANO

THE FRIENDS DON'T WANT TO HAVE TO FORK OUT AGAIN LIKE THEY DID LAST TIME. IT'S NO GOOD RELYING ON PEOPLE'S FINER INSTINCTS. RUN A LOTTERY INSTEAD – LOTTERIES ALWAYS MAKE LOTS OF MONEY – WITH A BIG CASH PRIZE – NOT SOME MINOR WORK BY A SECOND-RATE ARTIST.

H'MM! THE TRUSTEES HAVE BEEN USING GREENFIELD'S MONEY AS AN INVESTMENT FUND FOR NEARLY A CENTURY – NOW LET THEM REALISE SOME OF THEIR PROFITS! OF COURSE THEY CAN SELL A FEW PICTURES TO RAISE CASH – THEY CAN EASILY GET ROUND THE WILL.

BUSINESSMEN, BANKERS,
THE PRESS

WELL, LADIES AND GENTLEMEN, YOU ALL KNOW THE PROBLEM AND SOME OF THE POSSIBLE ANSWERS. WHAT SHOULD THE TRUSTEES DO?

45

VANILLA ISLAND
COCONUT GROVE

MAP 4 C1
3249
s/r $8-$12
rooms 42
(with
bath 34)
room
phones
TV lounge
ample free
parking
★★★ restaurant
owner:
Dick Jeffries

The Coconut Grove provides a splendid example of good hotel-keeping. Superb accommodation, friendly first-rate service. One of the best tables in the West Indies. Excellent amenities (swimming, sailing, surfing, tennis, golf). Super views.

Special features:

★ charismatic manager, Mr 'Sammy' Hall
★ fascinating mix of guests — employees from offshore oil-rigs, film directors, tycoons, rising local politicians, pop stars, treasure hunters, gold-diggers and of course plenty of locals
★ Mrs Sharma Singh's imaginative and versatile cooking. These succulent dishes — Caribbean and international — have made the restaurant a haven for gourmets. Service, wine, decor and ambience match the food.

HIGHLY RECOMMENDED

PROCLAIMED RESTAURANT OF THE YEAR!

THE CARIBBEAN ROOM AT THE COCONUT GROVE HOTEL

DINE AND DANCE TILL 2 AM

WHERE TO GO

WHAT TO DO

THE HARBOUR

A PLEASANT MORNING

Dick Jeffries' week had started well enough. Monday morning he had spent as usual at the Banana Marketing Board. Next, he had rung the hotel. Everything, naturally, was under control. 'What a stroke of genius', Dick thought, 'appointing Sammy Hall as manager of the Coconut Grove!' Thanks to that shrewd move, Dick had been able to concentrate on his real business interests, namely his engineering company and his part-time work for the Banana Board.

At lunch-time, he went to his club. Not unexpectedly, Paul Drew was already there when he arrived. Paul was the hotel's legal adviser and also Dick's personal friend. It was during the course of their meal that Paul came out with some very unwelcome news.

WARNING FROM A FRIEND

'You should spend more time at your hotel, Dick,' said Paul Drew. 'I know it's meant to be one of the best in the islands but . . .'

'Meant to be?' said Dick, sensing a hidden meaning in Paul's words. 'Do you honestly have any doubts about that?'

'I want to tell you something, off the record. Mind you, it's rather a delicate matter,' answered Paul.

Dick Jeffries began to feel uneasy. His friend was looking unusually serious. 'Come on, Paul, out with it.'

'OK. To put it bluntly, your boys in the bar are working some kind of racket. Fiddling the customers, and what's worse, cheating you.' Paul paused, looking rather uncomfortable himself.

'But it's not possible,' said Dick Jeffries. 'Sammy runs that bar in the evening. Surely you're not suggesting . . .'

'Look, Dick, I'll tell you what I know, and then you can judge for yourself.'

PAUL DREW'S STORY

Paul had suspected for some time that the hotel's bar employees were up to something. For one thing, a friend of his had commented that no one behind the bar seemed to know how to count properly. A dollar or two always seemed to get added to the bill, especially when large rounds were bought. 'Why didn't you mention it to Sammy?' Paul had asked. 'Don't make me

laugh. He makes even more mistakes than the two boys,' was the reply.

Paul had also noticed that the two barmen in question, Norman and Daryl, were spending money very freely. Norman had recently bought a sports car – very expensive in Vanilla because of the high import duty. Daryl was said to have the best hi-fi equipment in the town; he was also developing a taste for night life, and was frequently to be found in clubs, usually with a glamorous young lady in tow.

Suspicion that something was going on soon became certainty. Paul had undertaken some legal work for Jo Henry, the proprietor of a general store located near the hotel. In the course of conversation, Jo had said, 'Don't know what I'd do without the hotel. I must sell twenty or so bottles of the hard stuff to their bar every week. Norman or Daryl come in two or three times a

week, five o'clock on the dot. Good boys they are!'

'How long have they been doing that?' asked Paul, trying not to reveal his astonishment. 'Oh, for about two years now,' replied Jo Henry. 'Sammy also does the pick-up from time to time. What a character that fellow is, eh?'

'Indeed he is,' thought Paul to himself.

The information had staggered Paul. He knew for a fact that Dick Jeffries insisted on all alcoholic drinks being ordered from the local supermarket, because his brother was the owner. Paul was also aware of a well-known fiddle in the hotel trade. Some bar employees had been known to buy bottles of liquor, then serve customers from them, charging normal bar prices. A good profit could be made and, with luck, the hotel owner would know nothing about it.

CONFESSION OF A BARMAN

The two men dropped in to see Norman (the younger of the barmen) the following day. When informed that Daryl had 'confessed everything', poor Norman lost his nerve completely. Yes, they had been bringing in bottles of liquor and collecting the profit from them. But, Sammy Hall was the person to blame. He had put them up to it. Anyway, he always took 50 per cent of the evening's take, etc., etc.

Before the two men left, they made Norman promise to tell no one of their visit for the time being. He was also instructed to make up an excuse to be absent from the bar that evening.

As the two men walked away from Norman's apartment building towards their car, Dick Jeffries turned to his friend: 'Clever idea of yours, Paul, to pretend that Daryl had confessed. Now Norman has really let the cat out of the bag.'

DINNER ABOARD PAUL DREW'S YACHT

Later that evening, Dick Jeffries and his wife are having dinner with Paul and Sandra Drew. Because of the heat, the Drews have set up a table outside the boat's cabin so that they can eat in the open air. Dick is sipping his brandy moodily.

Dick Jeffries The whole problem is that the success of my hotel is almost entirely due to Sammy's efforts. He knows the business inside out. Do you know, Paul, we were hardly breaking even until Sammy came along. Now look at us. Things are really humming.

Paul Drew OK, he works like blazes at the job, and he's a tremendous personality, but he's been cheating you for over two years. Maybe he's been working other fiddles you don't know about.

Paula Jeffries If we throw Sam out, I wonder how long we'll keep Mrs Singh, our cook. Everyone knows that Sam and Mrs Singh are having an affair.

Sandra Drew That's right. There's another thing you must think of, Dick. Young Daryl's father works for the Tourist Department. How often do you think the Coconut Grove will be recommended to foreign visitors if you get rid of this boy? You've got to be realistic in these matters.

Paul Drew Well, I'm a lawyer and I like to have my facts presented clearly. Now, Dick, these are your options as I see them. Number one: you can turn a blind eye to the whole business, condone Sammy's and the barmen's cheating and forget I ever told you anything. Number two: fire Sammy – he seems to be the ringleader.

Dick Jeffries Well, yes, but we've already looked at that problem.

Paula Jeffries Don't forget, darling – we're sending Nicky to Cambridge next year, and we'll also have to fork out for Jane's wedding. All that's going to cost a bomb! Don't make any decisions you'll regret.

INSTRUCTIONS
Meet first in small groups of three or four people. Consider the options suggested by Paul Drew, and work out what other courses of action Dick Jeffries could take.

Then meet in one large group, with a chairman, and decide what you would advise Dick Jeffries to do.

TUMBRIL

TUMBRIL EDUCATIONAL PUBLISHING COMPANY

Until recently, Tumbril was a family business. The founder, Sir Hubert Tumbril, is still nominally Chairman, but management decisions are made by his son, Mr Richard Tumbril, and his nephew, Mr Jonathan Tumbril, who is Sales Director. Tumbril is now a public company, members of the family only holding 40 per cent of the equity. Nevertheless, there is still a family atmosphere in the organization.

THE FRANKFURT BOOK FAIR

Thanks to Jonathan's marketing flair and youthful energy – plus Richard's experience – the firm is doing well. Up to now, the bulk of sales has been in the UK; Tumbril has never paid much attention to selling abroad. However, its list of specialist titles in the social sciences and business field has begun to attract the attention of European schools and universities. At the last Frankfurt Book Fair, where they expected to do only modest business, the firm's stand was besieged with enquiries.

JONATHAN FINDS AN AGENT

Realizing that his staff could not handle a large volume of overseas business from their office near London, Jonathan made enquiries with a view to finding a reliable agent. He knew that the relationship between principal and agent is a peculiarly sensitive one in the book trade. It usually rests, not on a written contract, but on a gentlemen's agreement embodied in nothing more binding than a handful of letters confirming points made in informal discussions. If a publisher and his agent find they do not get on together, they generally part company with the least possible fuss. Neither side has much to gain by engaging in expensive legal action.

After sounding out a number of potential agents, Jonathan finally began talking seriously to Johan van Brasil NV, of Amsterdam. Van Brasil were just the people Jonathan had been looking for: a small office, but with a wide range of contacts in centres of learning throughout Europe; an old-fashioned attitude to business, but with most of the stock control and accounting handled by computer; a promising group of young sales staff, who travelled constantly and had shrewd ideas about what gaps were going to appear in the market for educational books. For their part, van Brasil were willing to discuss terms with Tumbril. Neither side was in a rush, so they agreed informally that the spring would be a good time for things to be finalized. Van Brasil could then take over the promotion and selling of Tumbril books, in Benelux only, for a trial period of one year.

RICHARD CLINCHES A DEAL

That was in the first days of January. Meanwhile, the Managing Director, Richard Tumbril, had gone on a private New Year visit to a friend in Stuttgart. On 4 January, Richard came back to the office and told Jonathan: 'Oh, Jonathan – I've got us an agent in Europe.'

'What do you mean, an agent in Europe? Van Brasil's going to be our agent, it's practically fixed.'

It turned out that Richard had met an American at a New Year's party in Germany. The American was the Vice-President of a chain of publishing houses which was buying up small European firms at a great rate. His latest acquisition was a German company called Gumpi, a

book distributor which had been in poor shape for years, but had once had a reputation in the academic book business.

The two men had agreed on a deal which seemed to promise great advantages for both Tumbril and Gumpi. The main points of the agreement were:

- Gumpi would take Tumbril's books on consignment, that is, on a sale or return basis. They would receive a commission of 20 per cent.
- Gumpi would not handle publications by Tumbril's British competitors.
- Tumbril would not deal with any other agent in Western Europe.
- The American undertook to bring Tumbril £500,000 worth of business inside two years.
- The agreement would run for two years.

When Jonathan heard about all this, there was nothing he could do except disentangle himself and the firm, with as little embarrassment as possible, from the arrangements he had made with van Brasil.

RUMOURS

In late March, a first shipment of books, worth £15,000, was on its way to Germany. At about that time, Jonathan began to hear disturbing rumours to the effect that the American's employers in the United States were not doing well. There were said to be lawsuits in progress against their subsidiaries for everything from tax evasion to the distribution of pornographic films. Jonathan did not panic unduly, however, because all seemed to be going well with Gumpi.

A TIME FOR ACTION

By the end of September, £80,000 worth of stock had passed through Gumpi's depot in Munich. Their monthly sales returns showed that the bulk of this stock had been distributed to booksellers. Another £55,000 worth was on its way from England and might already have arrived at the depot, so the American seemed to have every chance of exceeding his promised sales target.

Jonathan admitted this was good going, but he was by now extremely worried. Gumpi had by this time only made a token payment of £5,000 to Tumbril, and there were persistent rumours of the firm's impending bankruptcy. The first quarterly statement should have been settled by Gumpi at the end of July, but on 25 August, Tumbril got a letter from them asking for another six weeks in which to pay. That made even Richard feel very uneasy.

It is now 1 October. In the morning post, Richard Tumbril has received a letter that has thoroughly upset him. The American has written a brief note informing Richard that he has been recalled to the States. The letter ends: 'A colleague will be taking over from me. He will be busy for some while, but doubtless he will contact you in due course.'

FOUR POSSIBILITIES

'We'd better play this one by ear,' says Richard. 'The new man should be invited to come over here or perhaps I should go over there.'

'I don't think you should do that,' says Jonathan. 'Let's just recall all our stocks and get the hell out of it. If Gumpi goes broke, we may find it hard to get those books back, and the money they owe us will be shared among all the creditors. There's a Board meeting in two days' time. This Gumpi business can be put as an emergency item on the agenda.'

'Nice of you to put me in the picture beforehand, Jonathan,' says Mrs Fremlin, a powerful member of Tumbril's Board of Directors. 'There's only one thing to do now. We must cut loose from Gumpi with the minimum of fuss, and resume negotiations with van Brasil.'

'Damn stupid if you ask me,' says Peter Blandish from the Contracts Department. 'These agents are more trouble than they're worth. We ought to put one of our own people over there straight away – on a permanent basis. Jim Barker's doing well in our sales department. He's young, ambitious, speaks fluent German . . .'

INSTRUCTIONS

First, divide into small groups to analyse the problem and consider courses of action. Start by answering these questions:

(i) What factors created the present crisis?

(ii) What action should the company now take?

(iii) How can this kind of situation be avoided in the future?

Then, meet in one large group and decide what Tumbril should do to resolve the present crisis and to avoid similar problems in the future.

Hi-Flite

The organization chart of a successful department store
in a North London suburb.

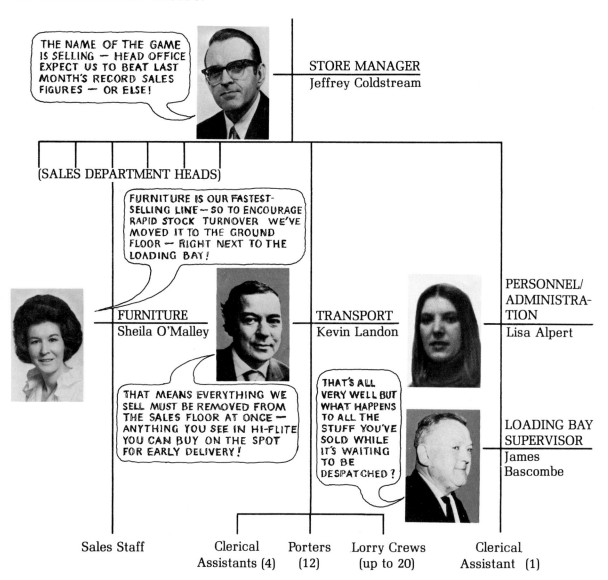

Unfortunately, the chart does not show the most important person
in the store — the customer.

BACKGROUND

Hi-Flite is the name of a group of department stores. Its head office is in Birmingham, and from there its Managing Director, John Fuller, keeps a watchful eye on the profitability of its forty-odd stores all over the UK.

To keep prices down, goods are bought in bulk and buying policy is therefore centralized. However, goods are delivered by wholesalers direct to Hi-Flite stores. There are no warehouses, since it is group policy to maintain rapid stock turnover and keep overheads to a minimum.

SUCCESS BRINGS PROBLEMS

The store that Fuller is especially concerned about at the moment is in North London. The North London Hi-Flite occupies premises which were purpose-built in the 1950s but which are now out of date and too small. There is no capital available for rebuilding, and every available square metre of floor space is required for selling and display. No reallocation of space is possible.

The North London Store Manager, Jeffrey Coldstream, has gone all out to develop the store's fastest-selling lines, which in this area are furniture, carpets and chinaware. The furniture department has been moved from the third floor down to street level, partly to attract customers and partly to make handling of heavy items easier. As soon as a piece is sold, it is not allowed to remain on show but is taken as quickly as possible to the Loading Bay to await delivery. The Loading Bay is small – 8 metres by 15 – but should be adequate, provided the space is properly used and delivery is not delayed.

The store has ten lorries, each with a crew of two: a driver and his mate. As a rule, a lorry makes one trip a day, loading up in the morning and dropping off items one by one to customers over a wide area in London and the Home Counties.

AN ANGRY PHONE CALL

All goods should be delivered within a week of purchase. But the reason Fuller is paying so much attention to North London is that he has recently had to deal with an unpleasant telephone call — from a very angry gentleman in Essex, who claims that he bought a bedroom suite in Hi-Flite and has been waiting for it for six weeks.

SOME REACTIONS FROM THE STAFF OF THE NORTH LONDON STORE

Jeffrey Coldstream (Store Manager) This must be cleared up at once. I'll get my PA to check how many complaints there've been, but meanwhile I'd better have a word with the people involved.

Sheila O'Malley (Furniture Department Manager) It's the penalty of success, I suppose. My job is to sell furniture. The Transport Department are supposed to deliver it. Kevin Landon's always on at the floor managers to push up their sales and keep stock moving. I know he's the blue-eyed boy and Head Office are grooming him for a seat on the Board or something, but it is his responsibility to get things on to the lorries and sent out. Why don't you ask him?

Kevin Landon (Transport Manager) Sure, I spend a lot of time on the sales floors. I don't see anything wrong in helping the sales staff to do their job – and that means moving stock around all the time, getting it out of the show-room, taking it through to the Loading Bay. Now that Loading Bay is a problem. It's always jampacked – no wonder things get damaged. You can never find anything, the documentation's so inefficient. Also, the porters aren't too careful, they bang about and bump into everything. They aren't *trained* to handle heavy items. As for the lorry crews – hopeless! They take their vehicles out half-empty and bring them back half-full. Mark you, I reckon Bascombe is a large part of the trouble. He still expects everyone to jump to attention and call him 'Sergeant'.

James Bascombe (Loading Bay Supervisor) Of course we have problems. To start with, there are more than twenty porters and drivers using that Loading Bay, but nobody really knows who they take their orders from. Mr Landon won't give them any instructions: says he's too busy elsewhere. Between you and me, sir, a lot of the lads are a bit inclined to laugh at him behind his back. But the porters and the lorry crews, they're not under me and they don't like me telling them what to do. So nobody really knows who's responsible for what. And the staff change so quick, half the time I don't even have a chance to learn their bloomin' names!

Ted Casson (driver's mate) Well, take me, for example. I came here a month ago and I'm thinking of asking for my cards. I mean, the pay's pretty rotten for a start. There's no incentive to do your work well – no training scheme – no prospects. And that Bascombe's a pain in the neck, always shouting at you when Mr Landon just lets you get on with it in your own way. Really, me and the rest are fed up – we get frustrated and I suppose we take it out on the furniture and things. Yes, well, it's just tough on the customer, I reckon.

Mary Venn (Store Manager's Personal Assistant) Here's a quick total for customers' complaints over the past six weeks, Mr Coldstream. You notice that complaints of late delivery or damage to goods are running at an average of over thirty a week!

INSTRUCTIONS

Working in small groups of three or four, analyse the reasons for the breakdown of Hi-Flite's storage and delivery systems. Is there a simple solution to the problem?

Then meet in one large group to decide what changes the Store Manager should make.

THE SCENE IS THE SULTANATE OF ... ...DE. FOR CENTURIES ITS PEOPLE HAVE LIVED THE LIFE OF THE DESERT, BREEDING FINE RACING CAMELS FOR THE NATIONAL SPORT.

BUT NOW, WITH THE COMING OF OIL...

A GLASS OF WATER, MR PRICE?

THANK YOU.

WE ARE NOT A LARGE COMPANY, MRS AL JABRI, BUT JUST FOR THAT REASON WE ARE NOT AFRAID TO TAKE A CALCULATED RISK.

SURE, I SPEAK FLUENT ARABIC - BUT I'VE DONE WELL HERE BECAUSE WE ALL SPEAK THE LANGUAGE OF PROFITABILITY.

IF YOU WANT TO SUCCEED IN THE SULTANATE, MR PRICE, YOU MUST KNOW HOW TO OPEN DOORS.

HMM...

AMONG MY PEOPLE, MR PRICE, WHERE FRIENDSHIP LEADS, BUSINESS WILL FOLLOW. BUT DON'T BE NAIVE! TALK IS CHEAP - IN EVERY COUNTRY.

QUITE SO.

THE COMPANY

Barnwood is a relatively new British company which makes laboratory glassware. Most of the firm's production goes to educational and industrial institutions in Britain, but Barnwood is now beginning to establish itself in carefully selected overseas markets. Laboratory equipment cannot be distributed in a mass market as if it were toothpaste; users' needs and the principal fields of research in a particular country have to be studied. The big buyers of laboratory equipment generally buy direct, and in the course of time close relationships often develop between the manufacturer and his major customers; smaller customers will go to a wholesaler or other distributor. In dealing with different countries, Barnwood employs whatever means of marketing and distribution seem most appropriate.

Like many exporters, Barnwood is interested in the market opportunities offered by the Middle East. The company made a few preliminary enquiries in Saudi Arabia and Iran some time ago. Then, at the end of last month, rather unexpectedly, it received a sizeable order for a specialized item of glassware from the research department of Codorah, an international corporation which has a plant in one of the Gulf states – we will call this state simply the Sultanate.

Acting on impulse, Mr Tom Price, Managing Director of Barnwood, followed up this order with a five-day sales trip to the Sultanate. Every evening, he jotted down in a notebook his impressions of the country and the results of meetings he had had during the day. These observations will help him and his colleagues to decide how to break into this Middle East market. In the pages that follow, you can read a number of extracts from Tom Price's notebook. First, however, you might like to read the major part of an article about the Sultanate which appeared recently on the financial page of a popular British newspaper.

OIL WEALTH BRINGS DEVELOPMENT TO GULF SULTANATE

FROM OUR SPECIAL CORRESPONDENT

Oil—$15 million worth every day—is providing the cash for the Sultanate's new five-year plan, announced by the Minister for Industry today.

"We don't want to be a one-resource economy for ever," the Minister told pressmen. "We want to diversify and build up our industrial sector. One day we may need to reduce our dependence on imports."

The plan provides for:

*More money to be invested in electric power, raw materials, housing, roads—the infrastructure of the country's economy

*The setting-up of a government fund to stimulate the development of private industry

*Massive investment in scientific and technical education at colleges and universities.

What does this really mean? Well, expect booming business conditions in the Sultanate and an all-out effort by the Government to make the country a leading Arab state in economic terms.

EXTRACTS FROM TOM PRICE'S NOTEBOOK

On his return, Tom Price's secretary typed up the notes he had made on meetings with key contacts.

June 7 (morning)

Met <u>Mrs Khalifa Al Jabri</u>

First woman in the country to become President of a company. Very good-looking, intelligent; dedicated to business and to the cause of women in the Sultanate.
'I hope that in ten years' time many other women will have reached positions comparable with mine.'
Member of a well-established family and a leading figure in society. Has political ambitions.

Runs the Hamed Al Jabri Trading Company which has a finger in every pie. Supplies labour, vehicles, equipment, to the oil companies. Builds car parks, shopping plazas, etc. Car distributorships, travel agency, import/export, and so on.

* She has an agency handling imported glassware, mainly kitchenware and ornamental. Distributes a limited amount of laboratory glassware, made by US and Eastern European firms, to schools and university science departments.

  Wants us to send out £60,000 worth of our goods on sale or return to assess its potential. Our glassware would be offered alongside competing products — not necessarily a bad thing, according to Mrs Al Jabri. Suggested 15 per cent commission would be acceptable. Said it would be a year before things started happening, but patience would bring rewards. Mentioned that she would be interested in acquiring the right to manufacture our goods under licence (paying us a royalty on each item sold).
  'It's good to get in at the beginning,' she said.

  Anything up her sleeve?

June 7 (afternoon)

Tea with <u>Mr Frank Bannerman</u>

General Manager of Codorah Corporation, manufacturer and wholesaler of pharmaceutical products.

Giant Texan, over two metres tall. Friendly, frank, energetic. Called himself a 'wheeler-dealer' type. Buccaneering.
'We Americans are all the same — trying to make one dollar into two.' (Roars with laughter.)
Has been in the Sultanate over ten years. Holds the blue card of Sultanate citizenship — a great honour for a foreigner.

His company operates on a joint-venture basis. Its president is a local man. US and European personnel supply expertise and hold many of the top jobs in the company.

   * Frank wants to be our 'contact' man. He will set up deals for Barnwood as time and opportunity permit.

     He has many contacts with companies, goverment departments, educational institutes, and so on. Claims to know many members of the famous 'fifteen families' who are said to have the real power in the country.

     Says Barnwood should 'think big' and forget about agents. We should get a few big contracts by any means possible, then open up our own sales office in the capital. Also said he would try to place further orders with us himself, but couldn't guarantee anything. Codorah only ordered from us on this occasion because the item in question was unobtainable locally.

     Frank wants an annual retainer fee of £3,000 plus 5 per cent commission on all deals. Arrangement to be reviewed after two years.

June 9

Met the <u>Junior Assistant to Deputy Minister for Industry</u>

Took me to watch national football team practise. Very self-assured man, articulate, ambitious. Immaculate dresser, but not ostentatious. 'Smooth', but much more impressive than I expected at first sight.

   * Told me <u>his</u> office granted import licences and revoked them. His people could also get goods released from customs when delays occurred (e.g. the Codorah order which was held up for six days on account of 'insufficient documentation') - a frequent occurrence apparently. His office can speed up paperwork.
    'If you want to succeed out here, Mr Price, you must know how to open doors.'

     Agents? Banking contacts? No problem! Many of his family are in business and financial circles.

     Also claims he has the ear of the Sultan.
    'All the cash here comes from the Goverment, that means the Sultan - right?'
    His final words were something like: 'You make it worth my while, Mr Price, and I'll see what I can do for you.'

June 11

Brief meeting in the new Convention Centre with <u>Mr Said Al Khalif, Minister for Industry</u>

He made these points:

- There are splendid opportunities for companies like ours, but it is 'easy to burn your fingers'.

- No simple recipe for success: necessary to be flexible.

- With Arabs, once friendship is established, business will follow.

- 'Don't be naive. Talk is very cheap here.'

INSTRUCTIONS

Divide into small groups of three or four people. Discuss the problems which would face most small firms trying to enter a market such as the Sultanate. Then, consider the merits and demerits of each proposal made to Tom Price during his sales trip.

Finally, meet as one large group under the guidance of a chairman. Decide what action – both immediate and long-term – Tom Price should take. You may wish to formulate an entirely new approach.

EASY GO

Businessman fined

Kuantan, Tuesday — An Australian businessman, William Anthony Merton, aged 32, appeared before magistrates here today, charged with being drunk and disorderly. It was stated that he had become involved in an argument and had made an unprovoked assault on Mr David Lim, a local businessman. Merton admitted the charges, but pleaded in his defence that he had been suffering from severe stress due to pressure of work and domestic problems. He is employed by the well-known Australian firm, Easy Go Marine of Sydney, and he has been touring Malaysia for the past five months setting up a franchise operation for Easy Go dealers. Merton was given a suspended sentence of three months in gaol, and was fined $750 and ordered to pay costs. A prosecution demand for his deportation from Malaysia was refused. AWB

EASY GO MEMO

From General Manager
To Head of Overseas Sales

Date 15 April
Ref pn/ jp/7

Bill Merton

The enclosed clipping was sent to me from an anonymous well-wisher in Kuala Lumpur.

It seems the story was syndicated by most of the Malaysian and Indonesian dailies, and of course everyone here in Sydney will soon hear all about it. Officially, we shall play the incident down — shrug it off as youthful high spirits and/or a trivial misunderstanding. If the press contact you, the line to take is 'No comment'.

In fact, of course, I am deeply concerned about the harm this story could do us in Southeast Asia, especially the more Moslem areas where people don't drink. I am also very worried about what is to become of Merton. The obvious answer is simply to recall him and replace him with someone else, but I would like your opinion before making any recommendation as to his transfer or dismissal.

EASY GO MEMO

From Head of Overseas Sales
To General Manager

Date 18 April
Ref rs/bp/17

Bill Merton

I feel strongly that Bill should be told to pull himself together and get on with the job in Malaysia. Basically, his problem is domestic and financial — his wife spends all her time shopping for bargains in Bangkok and Hong Kong. If he's got real financial problems, by all means let's reassess his salary and in the meantime pay his fine for him. But he was doing a first-class job in Malaysia until this happened; he's got all the local knowledge and personal contacts — which are what really count — and we've got no one else to touch him. In any case, the incident was hardly a serious one. I think we should be seen to support our staff in this kind of situation.

In my opinion, sacking Bill would help no one, least of all the company. We should show a little faith in him — maybe give him a little more financial and moral back-up than we have done in the past. I'm surprised we haven't had a letter from him yet, but no doubt we shall in a day or two.

Bob

A LETTER FROM BILL MERTON

RUSSELL HOTEL · SINGAPORE

16 April

Dear Bob,

I'm sending you, with this, my official report on the incident that took place in Kuantan a week ago. It was all a stupid mistake on my part. For some reason, I just blew my top, and started thumping a chap I met in a bar.

I suppose I should have cabled you earlier, but quite honestly I've been feeling pretty bad these last few days. The local doctor has prescribed tranquillizers for me. I'm not sure they'll help much, though. My real problem — or part of it anyway — is Belinda. If I could get things sorted out with her, I should be OK again.

Really, Malaysia has been an unlucky place for me. My marriage began to crack up over here. Somehow, everything seems to have got a bit too much for me. Apart from Belinda, another problem is that I've been out on a limb here for months, trying to do a decent job of work when no one back home cares a damn. I don't seem to have any back-up at all. For example, take that demonstration model of the new motor I ordered. What on earth's happened to it? And my expense account hasn't been paid since January. It's just not good enough. I've worked hard over here. I reckon I've done six months' work in three months, but all that happens is that people in Sydney start telling stories about my drinking habits. They're not true, of course, but I'm stuck here and can't defend myself.

I wonder if you could do me a favour. I want you to suggest to Jason Porter that I should have two or three months' sick leave. I need time to get my own life organized. I shall be going up to Malacca next week. Belinda is meeting me there. I'd love to be able to give her a surprise — a second honeymoon in Kashmir, perhaps! She's always complaining that I put the company first and her second — I think that's one reason she behaves the way she does. You can cable me in Malacca next Friday, c/o the Ocean Front Hotel.

All the best now,
Yours,
Bill Merton

DISCUSSING BILL'S FUTURE

After reading Bill's letter and the report, Jason Porter – Easy Go's General Manager – discusses the problem with the Head of Overseas Sales, Bob Pickup.

Bob Well – what do you make of it?

Jason His report doesn't tell us much that we didn't already know. The letter to you, though – that's another matter. It's full of self-pity. I can't stand that sort of thing. He's got to snap out of it.

Bob Maybe, but I've always thought of Bill as being very tough-minded, independent. In this letter, he seems to be accusing us, as if we've let him down in some way. And he's certainly not usually a heavy drinker.

Jason Now you listen to me, Bob. We picked Bill Merton to handle this franchising operation in Malaysia. True, he wasn't totally committed to the project, but that's beside the point. He's just got to pull himself together now and see the job through.

Bob I think you're being very hard on him. He's a very sensitive person, you know.

Jason Sensitive? I'd say a lot of people find Bill aggressive and conceited. He puts people's backs up, or he can do. I'm not at all surprised he's having marital problems.

Bob Oh, come on, Jason. Would you like your wife to spend money the way Belinda does?

Jason Look, basically Belinda resents the amount of time Bill gives to the company. She's bored and lonely, so she makes up for it by spending money. Anyway, don't feel too sorry for Bill. We're paying him a pretty good salary.

Bob Yes, but for a very tough and wearing job, let's face it. Well, as I see it, there seem to be several things we can do. One: ask Bill to give in his resignation. Then, we'd have to find someone to replace him. Two: give him what he's asked for – three months' sick leave on full pay. That'd put our franchising operation completely out of phase, of course. Three: keep him where he is. Allocate funds – and personnel too, if need be – to support him. Only we don't know how much that might cost. Four: call him back here and replace him with someone else.

Jason There is a fifth possibility. As you know, Bill was never keen on our franchising programme for Malaysia. He wanted a centralized distribution network, based on a subsidiary marketing company in Kuala Lumpur. It would mean undoing all the work he's done, but no franchising agreements have actually been signed yet.

INSTRUCTIONS

First, divide into small groups and try to answer these questions:

(i) What sort of person is Bill Merton really?

(ii) How closely ought Head Office to monitor and control Merton's activities in Malaysia?

(iii) How long can Head Office postpone making a final decision about Merton's future?

(iv) What would be the implications of abandoning the franchise programme in Malaysia and setting up a marketing subsidiary instead?

Finally, meet as one group. Discuss your answers to the above questions, then decide what to do about Bill Merton, and what sort of telegram (if any) should be sent to him at the Ocean Front Hotel, Malacca.

MACQUILTER

A Canadian golf-club manufacturer is dissatisfied with its export performance in Japan. It must adopt a new marketing strategy to boost sales in that country.

GETTING DOWN TO BUSINESS ON THE EIGHTEENTH GREEN

The scene is the Longacre Golf Club, Toronto. Two men are on the green, about to putt. They are Herbie Young and Hiroshi Kato, who is a well-known golfing professional in Japan. Herbie has been complaining about Macquilter's poor sales record in Japan.

Hiroshi So – can't you change your marketing approach?

Herbie Well, we've got to change something. Your country's the second biggest market in the world for golf equipment. But it's a rough market. The competition's murder. OK, Hiroshi, your putt, I think. Must be a good fifteen feet. Nice one! You sure know how to put them in.

Hiroshi Come on – I almost missed it, you know.

Herbie You're not trying to tell me you're worried about your game, Hiroshi?

Hiroshi It's certainly not what it used to be. I don't look it perhaps, but I'm forty-four now. That's rather old for professional golf; anyway, too old for the big tournaments. But I know plenty of people in the golfing world, especially in my country. I wondered if maybe I could be useful to you?

Herbie You mean, marketing Macquilter products over there?

Hiroshi Why not? It's true, I'd need some training; I've not had much business experience. But, suppose you made me your agent – I couldn't do much worse than you're doing at the moment, and I might well do a lot better.

Herbie How serious are you about this, Hiroshi?

Hiroshi Well, as you know, I came to Canada to talk about the clubs I'll need for next season. But, let's face it, time's running out for me. Next season could be my last.

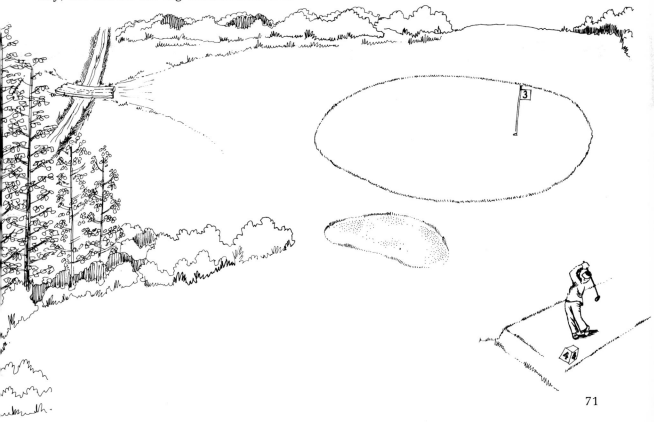

THE COMPANY AND ITS PRODUCTS

Macquilter make a comprehensive range of woods, irons and putters, each design being manufactured in several different sizes and weights. Left-handed and ladies' clubs are available, and the firm is always willing to make up custom-built sets – at a price.

Each year one or two designs are dropped from the range and replaced by new ones. The golfing world is acutely fashion-conscious. Every golfer is seeking that wonder club which, he is convinced, will put extra power into his drive or help him knock a stroke or two off his handicap. The golf course is a place where people like to impress each other with their style, smartness and taste. Because of this, Macquilter make fifteen designs of golf bag, as well as golf trolleys and a high-priced range of golf balls. There are also Macquilter shoes, sweaters and other clothing.

MARKETS

Since 1973, when Herbie Young became Executive Vice-President, Macquilter have greatly developed their export business, using the technique of making intensive efforts in carefully selected markets. One wise decision was to concentrate on European markets rather than on the huge but highly competitive US market. As a result, the company's exports to Germany, France and Scandinavian countries are now large. It is also achieving a useful market share in other European countries.

Last year, total annual sales amounted to almost six million dollars, 60 per cent of this being accounted for by export earnings outside the North American continent.

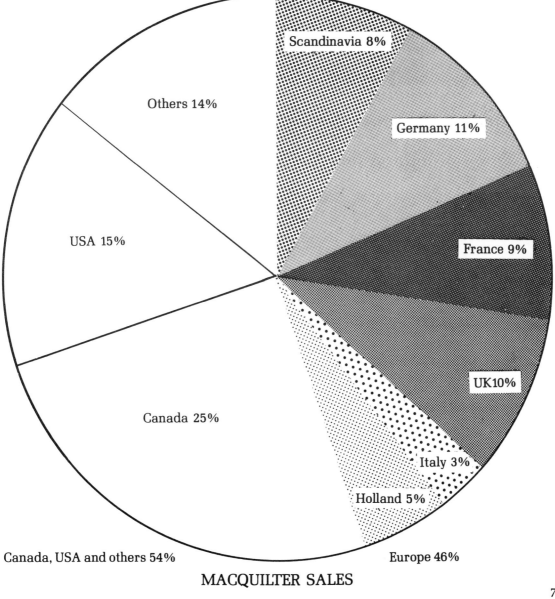

Scandinavia 8%

Others 14%

Germany 11%

USA 15%

France 9%

UK 10%

Canada 25%

Italy 3%

Holland 5%

Canada, USA and others 54%

Europe 46%

MACQUILTER SALES

WORKING OUT STRATEGIES

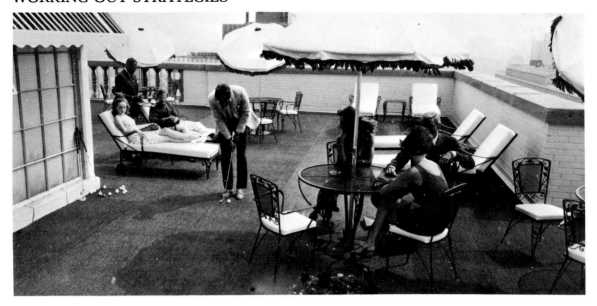

Some weeks later, Herbie Young is in the open-air bar on the roof of the Park Plaza Hotel. This bar is a favourite haunt of golf addicts who can practise their putting on the heavy green carpet at one end of the bar. With Herbie are two other Macquilter executives, Frank Boyers and Eric Weiss, heads of marketing and finance respectively.

The three men argue heatedly about the Japanese market. All agree that the present agent must go. However, they have different ideas about how sales should be expanded in Japan. Later, Herbie Young summarized the three proposals made during their discussion. Here are his typed-up notes:

---

1 <u>Make a deal with Hiroshi Kato</u>

The best solution, in my opinion. I've talked a lot with Hiroshi — am very impressed. He knows exactly what he wants:

- one month's training at our factory (and at our expense)

- a three-year exclusive agency agreement (give him time to show what he can do)

- 12 per cent commission (our present agent gets 10 per cent)

- Macquilter to pay half the costs of advertising and ware-housing when sales have built up to an agreed level

- generous expense account.

Hiroshi's strategy: he wants to start by persuading club professionals to carry Macquilter stock (negotiating exclusive contracts where possible). He also intends to persuade manufacturers to make Macquilter clothing, equipment, etc. under licence — has already sounded out a company in Nagasaki, who are very interested.

---

2 <u>Negotiate with Toshi Kakimoto</u>

Frank Boyers' idea. He is convinced Kakimoto would do business with us on
favourable terms. Successful businessman — already owns medium-sized factory making golfing equipment, and wholesale business distributing a wide
range of products, his own and other manufacturers'. Also owns several
sports shops in big cities.

Points Kakimoto made to Frank on Frank's last trip:

- present agent concentrates too much on department stores.
  In Japan, most golf clubs etc., are sold in specialist
  sport shops — a fair number by professionals

- he would purchase clubs and balls direct from us; hold
  stock, advertise and distribute at his own expense

- he would <u>not</u> want an exclusive agreement (he handles
  stuff from many other makers)

- he would negotiate a fixed-price contract each year
  (Frank couldn't shake him on this)

- he would produce Macquilter golf bags and trolleys in
  Japan under licence; complains they are too bulky to
  ship from Canada.

3 <u>Set up a franchise operation</u>

Eric Weiss strongly in favour. We've received numerous letters from
Japanese dealers wanting to handle our products. Under this scheme,
<u>all</u> retail outlets would be franchised shops. Each franchisee would:

- sell Macquilter-approved goods only

- invest a substantial sum of his own capital in the business

- pay Macquilter for the use of the name and for the initial
  training, promotional assistance, etc. that we would
  provide

- pay an annual royalty based on purchases of goods from us
  (perhaps 5 per cent to start with?)

- ensure that his shop decor and display conformed to a
  standardized company image.

The franchisee would get help in display techniques, would enjoy the benefit
of national advertising (paid for by us), and would be granted credit facilities to buy stock — but the important point is that he would be <u>in business
on his own account</u>; charging whatever prices the market would bear.

INSTRUCTIONS

First, meet in small groups of three or four
people and discuss the three proposed
solutions to Herbie Young's problem. Consider their advantages and disadvantages,
and the likely effects of each, both in the
short and in the long term.

Then, meeting as one large group,
decide what Macquilter should do in order
to improve their performance in the Japanese market.

WESTMEATH

A WORRIED TELEPHONE CALL

'Get me Stockholm, will you.' Fergus McLaren did not need to tell his secretary who he wanted to speak to. Fredriksen, the boss of Karlstad-Poly, sounded cross at being called out of a management meeting, but McLaren was in no mood to apologize. 'We've got problems,' he said curtly. 'There's a rumour going around the factory that Karlstad are going to put all the people at Westmeath out of work in six months. Everything's going to be made by robots . . . Yes, of course! That's exactly what I told them: no decision has been made yet, interests of the workforce will be safeguarded, etc., etc. However, my workers can read the local paper just as well as I can, and that's where the rumours have started. I've now got about twenty people out on unofficial strike, with the unions breathing down my neck and threatening to make it official if they don't receive categorical assurances from Karlstad-Poly that there will be no redundancies for at least eighteen months. Now then – are you in a position to give such assurances?'

There was a brief pause. Then: 'I'll ring you back,' Fredriksen said. 'Just play for time.' And he hung up.

THE COMING OF THE SILICON CHIP

For many years it has been the policy of the government of the Republic of Ireland to develop and diversify the country's economy. As a result, many foreign companies have established themselves there, with active encouragement from Dublin. Overseas investment means more jobs and better pay for Irish workers. The government did not object, therefore when Westmeath Kitchen Equipment announced a few months ago that 80 per cent of the shares in the company were to be sold to the big Swedish group, Karlstad-Poly. Union representatives and the two worker-directors on the board of Westmeath raised no objection either. Karlstad-Poly let it be known that they would expand production capacity and increase wages.

Shortly after the Karlstad takeover, however, there was a shift in the balance of power among the top management in Stockholm. New and more abrasive policies were formulated for the group. It became abundantly clear that all production and management systems would from then on be expected to keep pace with every technological advance, particularly in the field of micro-electronics, data processing and automatic process control. Massive capital investment programmes had already been announced for the group's subsidiaries in several countries, and Westmeath managers, though they had not yet heard anything from Stockholm directly, suspected that they too were going to be affected before much longer.

McLaren's attitude, and that of most of his colleagues, was cautious. They all knew that change must come sometime; they accepted the arguments that increased productivity must make the company healthier and might lead to more jobs – eventually. But how radically the pattern of employment would change, and how long it would take to overcome the first shock of the new technology, was still quite unpredictable.

A FALSE ALARM?

The atmosphere at Westmeath was therefore somewhat uneasy, even before the publication of a sensational article in the *Clonderry Advertiser*. Someone had evidently been leaking information, reliable or otherwise, to business correspondents of the Irish press, who lost no time in spelling out the implications. In the words of Brian Caskell, of the *Advertiser*:

It appears that Karlstad-Poly will shortly make known its requirements to Westmeath Kitchen Equipment regarding the modernization of its factory. These are expected to include:

- redesign and retooling of the company's premises on the Clonderry Industrial Estate
- drastic reduction of Westmeath's product range to facilitate the programming of the central computers
- massive cuts in the Clonderry labour force, up to five-sixths of whom can expect to find themselves unemployed within two years.

The impact on Clonderry looks like arousing considerable controversy.

'Alarmist rubbish,' was Managing Director McLaren's reaction when an agitated shop steward waved Caskell's article at him in the office next day. 'I've no reason whatever to believe that anyone will be laid off. Don't worry; as soon as anyone knows anything definite, you'll be informed.'

'Just as I thought,' said the shop steward. 'You're as much in the dark as we are.' McLaren realized he had made a tactical error, but he had been thrown off guard by seeing a diagram that the man was carrying in his other hand. Apparently it was to be photocopied and put up on factory and canteen notice boards. It illustrated, all too vividly, what the new technology might mean to Westmeath.

ROBOTS - WHAT THEY WILL MEAN TO YOU

Westmeath Kitchen Equipment Ltd is now controlled by the giant Swedish combine, Karlstad-Poly. Karlstad-Poly intend to spend over £1m to introduce Advanced Process Control systems here in our factory. That means that a lot of jobs will be taken over and given to machines controlled by computers and micro-circuits. We, the workers' representatives, believe that full implementation of Karlstad-Poly's plans would lead very quickly to the situation shown below.

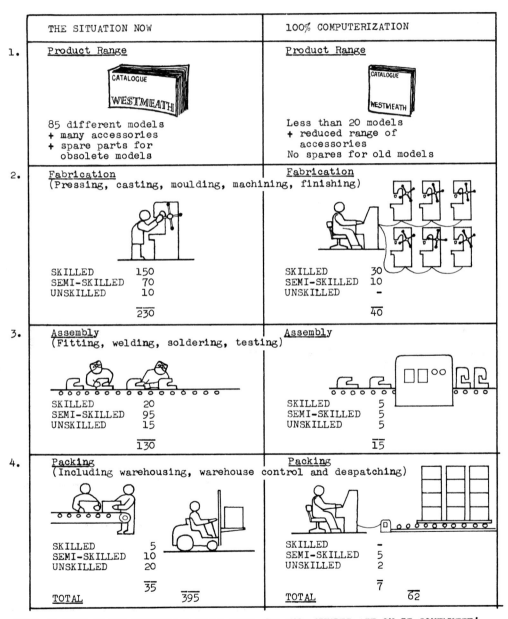

	THE SITUATION NOW	100% COMPUTERIZATION
1.	**Product Range** 85 different models + many accessories + spare parts for obsolete models	**Product Range** Less than 20 models + reduced range of accessories No spares for old models
2.	**Fabrication** (Pressing, casting, moulding, machining, finishing) SKILLED 150 SEMI-SKILLED 70 UNSKILLED 10 ___ 230	**Fabrication** SKILLED 30 SEMI-SKILLED 10 UNSKILLED - ___ 40
3.	**Assembly** (Fitting, welding, soldering, testing) SKILLED 20 SEMI-SKILLED 95 UNSKILLED 15 ___ 130	**Assembly** SKILLED 5 SEMI-SKILLED 5 UNSKILLED 5 ___ 15
4.	**Packing** (Including warehousing, warehouse control and despatching) SKILLED 5 SEMI-SKILLED 10 UNSKILLED 20 ___ 35 TOTAL 395	**Packing** SKILLED - SEMI-SKILLED 5 UNSKILLED 2 ___ 7 TOTAL 62

LOOK AT THIS CHART CAREFULLY: YOUR NAME AND SHOP NUMBER ARE ON IT SOMEWHERE!

HINTING AT A COMPROMISE

'Hard day at the office?' asks Alice McLaren sympathetically when her husband comes home.

'Average,' says Fergus, and he explains to her why there are twenty workers on unofficial strike.

'I saw something in the local paper about it,' she says. 'You'd better be ready for trouble if it comes, hadn't you?'

'Well, all the managers are arguing over what attitude to take. Do we stand firm, or give way, or what? Of course, the result will be the same in the long run – but labour relations in the next five years are going to be a lot harder if we do the wrong thing now.'

'In any case, the people in Stockholm will have to listen to you!' says Alice in disgust. 'Just tell them, no!'

'Ah, you're talking as if it was all or nothing,' says Fergus. 'But we'll probably end up with some stupid compromise that satisfies nobody. Like the computer takes half the factory and the workforce keeps the other half; that sort of thing.'

'But your workers are highly skilled! No computer can do a craftsman's job. And the unions wouldn't stand for it.'

'There may not be many more craftsmen's jobs, and the unions may not have much say in the matter. Anyway, by no means everyone in the factory is a craftsman. The ones who are on strike at the moment are mostly unskilled. Even if their union gives them official backing, it's not the same union as the one the craftsmen belong to. As for the semi-skilled people, they're mostly part-timers and very few of them carry union cards at all.'

'Then,' says Alice, 'all you've got to do is to schedule the computer takeover very carefully. This year: packing department. Next year: assembly. Or this year: unskilled jobs. Next year: semi-skilled jobs. And so on. Well, the unions ought to agree to that. You can't stand in the way of progress, after all.'

INSTRUCTIONS

There seem, so far, to be four courses of action that Westmeath can follow:

(i) accept automatic process control and computerization, as and when Karlstad-Poly require it to be introduced and make the necessary capital available

(ii) seek by every possible means to dissuade or prevent Karlstad-Poly from installing any new technology that may lead to redundancies among the workforce

(iii) negotiate with Karlstad-Poly, with a view to limiting the extent of computerization; thus, only certain areas of the factory, or certain processes or types of job, would be affected

(iv) negotiate, with a view to staggering the coming of automation over a period of perhaps seven years, so that redundancies and other labour problems do not come all at once.

Meet in small groups to discuss the likely effects and repercussions of each of these policies.

Then, in one large group, decide what line Westmeath should take, and what Fergus McLaren should tell Fredriksen the next time he telephones him.

AT THE ZURICH FAIR

It is the final day of 'British Week' in Zurich. The chairman of a small company has flown in for the day to see how his firm's stand has been doing. In the late afternoon, one of his biggest Swiss customers drops by for a chat.

Sanderson Yes, our sales in Switzerland are up 70 per cent on last year. We'll soon top a quarter of a million pounds' turnover.

Duthli Well, the quality is high and we know your delivery dates can be relied on. That's something.

Sanderson You don't sound very impressed.

Duthli To speak frankly, Mr Sanderson, you're not doing nearly as well as you should be. Some of your designs will never sell in Europe – but you keep on trying to promote them.

Sanderson Yes, I know. Like those ski-caps that were such a fiasco. Well, you can't win them all. My target is a fifty per cent increase in sales each year for five years. Then we'll set up our own subsidiary right here in Zurich.

Duthli Listen. Long before that time, big manufacturers in other countries will drive you out of the market. They'll match you in quality and price, but they'll have better designs and better marketing. Believe me – I speak as a friend, Mr Sanderson: if Tanskin does not establish itself as one of the market leaders in Switzerland within two or three years, then you're out – finished!

A PROBLEM WITH SALES IN SWITZERLAND

ON HIS WAY HOME FROM ZURICH

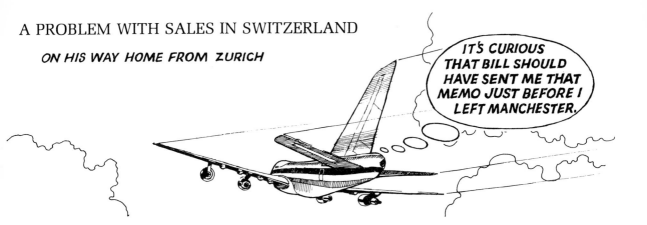

TANSKIN

FROM Marketing Director   TO Chairman

DATE 28 July   REF cd/ww/11

SUBJECT   <u>Overseas Marketing</u>

1 In view of the increasing importance of the Company's sales overseas,
I believe that a gap may shortly become apparent in our organization. I
refer particularly to Switzerland, which now accounts for 12 per cent of
our total sales and which is likely to become of much greater importance
to us in the future. I am convinced that however vigorously our sales
effort in that country is led from Head Office, this will never be as
effective as a full-time representative on the spot.

2 I should therefore like to propose that this matter be included in the
agenda for the next meeting of the Board. Briefly, what I would like to
see is a new post of Export Salesman, reporting to the Export Manager,
but located permanently in Switzerland and preferably a Swiss national.
If we can find the right man (or woman), it may be possible to groom him
as a future head of our European sales subsidiary.

WHAT KIND OF MANAGER?

When he arrives at Ringway Airport, Manchester, Derek Sanderson is surprised to be met by his Production Manager, Alfred Blunt.

As they drive along the M56 motorway:

Sanderson I think we've got a tremendous opportunity in Switzerland, Fred. We could be poised for a real breakthrough. Do you reckon the factory could cope?

Blunt Oh, we can make them all right if the sales people can sell them. Frankly, I'm a bit tired of having production schedules messed about because Arthur suddenly realizes at the last moment he can't get anyone outside the UK to buy one of his special lines. I mean, look at that nonsense with the ski-caps.

Sanderson Yes, that was mentioned in Zurich. But I can't blame Arthur for that.

Blunt Oh no, I'm not criticizing anyone – not behind his back.

Sanderson Arthur's no ball of fire, I know – but he's been selling for twenty years, four years in the export business . . .

Blunt Knives and forks, wasn't it? In Mexico.

Sanderson Well – cutlery, kitchenware – mostly in Latin America, I admit, but he's worked very hard to research our potential markets, he's got bags of energy and he's a first-rate organizer. . . . I wonder, though, if we need someone in the job who's got a better design background? Looking at the other exhibits in Zurich, I must say I realized how traditional some of our stuff looks. Anyone who knew about design wouldn't have even tried to sell those ski-caps abroad.

Blunt Well, good luck, Derek; the sort of man you need in that job isn't going to be content with what you pay Arthur, though. Could cost you another three or four thousand a year on his salary, just for a start.

Organization Chart: Tanskin Ltd

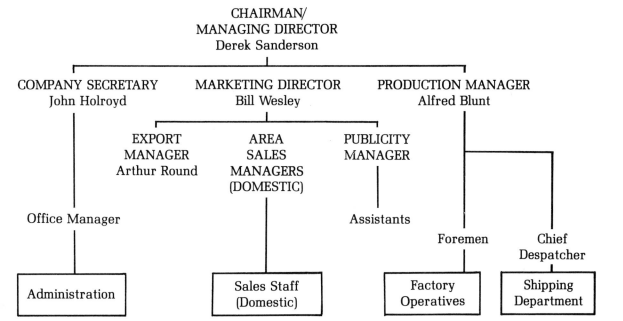

IMPROVING THE SITUATION

A few days later, a meeting is called by Sanderson to discuss ways in which the Tanskin management team can reduce expenditure.

John Holroyd (Company Secretary) Could I make one other point, Derek? I think it's fair to say that we all attach great importance to our sales effort abroad – I'm thinking especially of Switzerland – and quite rightly we devote substantial funds to promoting Tanskin's products in that market. At the same time, I'm a little doubtful as to the advisability of operating, as we have done so far, at such a distance from our customers. You've just been to Zurich – fair enough – but with respect, I do feel that the repeated visits made by the management throughout the year represent a drain on our resources that we can ill afford.

Arthur Round (Export Manager) I presume that John is referring to my activities in Switzerland – and elsewhere.

Sanderson Four or five days in Zurich costs the firm less than a thousand pounds, all in. When you think that our sales there are well over two *hundred* thousand . . .

Holroyd Yes, but let's face it: our sales are good because our profit margins are very low. Our *net* profit from exporting last year wasn't much over ten thousand pounds.

Round Well – we're preparing the ground still. Rome wasn't built in a day.

Holroyd No – but it got built, in the end. I really wonder, Derek, if we wouldn't do better to use an agent in Switzerland.

Round An agent? But then we'd be paying commission.

Holroyd Yes, but the improvement in sales might well justify it.

Sanderson We've never used an agent anywhere. They may be fine for all sorts of businesses, but I'm not so sure about our case. I've heard stories about agents that would make your hair stand on end. Embezzlement, bankruptcy . . . What sort of agent were you thinking of, anyway?

Holroyd OK, OK – it was just a suggestion. As Company Secretary, I daresay I was speaking out of turn. I just think that maybe we're using the wrong sales method in Switzerland – that's all.

ARTHUR ROUND'S REACTION

A day or two later, the Export Manager, Arthur Round, departs on another foreign trip, this time to Scandinavia. Not long afterwards, the following letter arrives for Derek Sanderson.

Stockholm, 9 August

Dear Derek,

I have been giving a good deal of thought to the topic that came up at the last management meeting and I feel compelled to let you know what my conclusions are. Although I know you will not take any decisions in my absence, I also know from experience how opinions can 'firm up' very quickly, and I want to add my contribution right away to the debate about export marketing.

As you know, I believe that gradual development of overseas markets is advisable, for a number of reasons. However, if a very rapid expansion is felt to be unavoidable, then it seems to me that Tanskin is using the wrong marketing approach. Far quicker progress could be made by setting up a full-scale Export Department in the firm, with a staff of three or four people who would concentrate on researching markets, making contact with buyers, following up enquiries and orders, handling paper-work and dealing with problems of finance.

I believe that this is the only way in which the company could tackle the enormous volume of work that rapid growth abroad would entail – but I look forward to discussing it with you when I return from Scandinavia next week. As you know, I worked with a department of this sort in my previous job. I am convinced the market potential in Scandinavia alone would more than justify the expense of staff, premises and equipment. Yesterday

INSTRUCTIONS

Your job, as management consultants, is to advise Derek Sanderson and Tanskin on the firm's best course of action. Here is a summary of the four suggestions that have been put forward so far. Tanskin can

(i) replace the present Export Manager with a Manager who has good qualifications in industrial design as well as varied export experience

(ii) use an agent in Switzerland

(iii) create the position of Export Salesman (Switzerland)

(iv) set up a special Export Department at the company's headquarters in Manchester.

Tanskin can meet the cost of any one of these proposals. But it cannot afford to follow up more than one – and it cannot afford to make a mistake.

First, get together in four small groups (one for each proposal) and work out the probable consequences of your group's proposal being accepted. What costs would be incurred? What changes would have to be made in the company's organization or strategy? What management or personnel problems might arise as a result?

Then meet as one group for the final discussion, and choose the right course of action for Tanskin.

DECREE NO.2 OF THE MILITARY GOVERNMENT OF THE REPUBLIC OF BAKUMBA

Schedule 3: 40 per cent BAKUMBAN OWNERSHIP

1 Advertising
2 Assembly of radio and television receivers and other domestic electrical appliances
3 Blending and bottling of alcoholic drinks
4 Boat-building
5 Bottling and/or canning of soft drinks
6 Clearing and forwarding agents
7 Canning and preserving of fruit and vegetables
8 Coal mining and distribution
9 Dry-cleaning and valeting services
10 Dyeing and colour processing of fabrics

BACKGROUND

For many years, the Blik Corporation has successfully marketed its soft drinks on a worldwide scale. Its sales do not compare with those of the other big multinational soft-drink companies, but it does pretty well. Blik has a secret formula which gives it its distinctive and inimitable flavour.

This formula is known only to a small group of skilled technicians, appointed by Head Office, in each area of the world where Blik operates. Even Area Managers do not always know it. The syrup which is produced from the formula is sent to bottling plants run by licensees and subsidiaries; they dilute it with carbonated water and distribute it.

Many African countries, taking their lead from Nigeria, are beginning to insist that foreign businesses must be indigenized – that is, they must be partially or wholly owned by nationals of the country in which they are located. Often, senior management must likewise be in the hands of local people.

Blik is quite sympathetic to this idea in principle, but in practice the Corporation continues to be highly centralized and a tight rein is kept on area offices. This inevitably leads to the appointment of a high proportion of Americans to senior posts in almost all areas. The secret formula is an additional problem: the Board are always worried about the possibility of it falling into the wrong hands or being sold to local competitors.

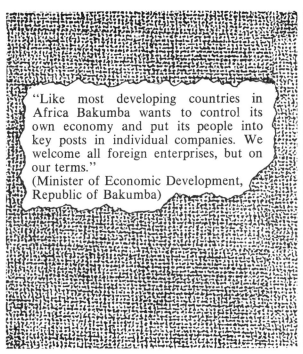

"Like most developing countries in Africa Bakumba wants to control its own economy and put its people into key posts in individual companies. We welcome all foreign enterprises, but on our terms."
(Minister of Economic Development, Republic of Bakumba)

The latest indigenization decree

By DAVID SYLVESTER, recently in Bakumba

The latest decree of the Bakumban Government represents a further stage in the indigenization of the country's economy. This policy means, essentially, that all businesses will become either partially or wholly owned by Bakumbans.

By the terms of this decree, some foreign companies which previously had to become at least 40% Bakumban-owned now find themselves moved into the 60% category. These companies will have to sell a further 20% of their equity to comply with the decree.

A further group of foreign companies find that, for the first time, they are subject to the provisions of this type of decree, and must offer 40% of their shares to the Bakumban public. For example, the well-known soft-drinks manufacturer, Blik Corporation, is now in this position.

ECONOMIC NATIONALISM

This indigenization is only part of the policy of economic nationalism pursued since the end of the Civil War in 1976 and which accelerated after the military coup in 1978. Other elements are oil policies and labour permit policy.

The Bakumban policy towards foreign oil companies is fairly restrictive. The effective profit tax is over 90% and the exploration interest has been taken over by the Bakumba National Oil Corporation.

Even more restrictive is the current labour permit policy. There has been constant pressure on companies to reduce the number of expatriate staff. One large US bank employing only 30 to 40 expatriates was nevertheless instructed to reduce their number by one third.

THE PROBLEM

The Military Government of the central African state of Bakumba formally instituted a policy of indigenization in 1976, but Blik had expected to escape for some years to come. The new decree, putting Blik into the 40 per cent category, has caused a good deal of commotion in the Corporation. Later this week, the senior executives of Blik (Bakumba) are going to meet representatives from Head Office in order to discuss what line they should take.

Three currents of opinion seem to be emerging from the buzz of rumour, gossip and controversy. These approaches are outlined below:

1 Blik should pull out of Bakumba

The Corporation should abandon its operations in Bakumba altogether. The Bakumbans will soon be demanding 60 per cent, then 100 per cent – so it is argued. Although turnover is good (close to US$10m last year, and rising by about 15 per cent a year), Blik's share of the cola market is steady at around 18 per cent and profitability is low. A few years ago, a lot of money was put into three bottling plants. These ultra-modern automated plants are still not working to capacity, but interest rates on loans, plus high distribution expenses, are eating into profits. Sale of the plants might realize anything up to US$8m, though how much of that money could be remitted to the US is uncertain. Pulling out will ensure the Corporation keeps the secret formula of Blik. Despite official denials, it is thought the Blik bosses in Chicago are in favour of this course of action.

2 Blik should cooperate with the Government

Blik (Bakumba) should conform, without a struggle, to the decree. This would mean that Blik would have to sell 40 per cent of its shares on the Bakumban Stock Exchange at prices decided by the Bakumban Issues Commission (BIC). So far, BIC's valuations of shares have tended to err very much on the low side. As for the formula of the drink, it is argued that in this age of sophisticated industrial espionage technology, this will not remain secret very much longer. Since the policy of indigenization is spreading throughout developing countries, the Corporation will ultimately be unable to keep the formula secret. A policy of cooperation at this stage will win Blik much official goodwill. It will, of course, also lead to Bakumbans occupying many senior posts, including possibly that of President. It has always been Blik's policy to train nationals to take over certain jobs, but it does not expect to have many suitably qualified Bakumban staff for another three to five years.

3 Blik should resist the Government's demands

Blik (USA) should support Blik (Bakumba) in putting up the stiffest possible fight. The bottling plants and distribution system provide work for some 4,000 people in areas where unemployment is high. If Blik pulled out, the governments of the provinces where the plants are located would lose quite substantial amounts in local taxes and interest on loans, while they and the central government would lose foreign currency payments and the chance of future capital investment. Blik should put strong pressure on the Government, arguing that the formula is essential to its commercial success, and that therefore the Corporation must be 100 per cent American-owned.

AN EXPERT OPINION

On the day before Julius Feinburg, Vice-President of Blik (Bakumba), is due to meet his Chicago bosses, he receives this letter from his friend Hanna Mrozek, a Czechoslovakian economist who is an expert on the Bakumban economy.

Lagos Airport
1 Sept

Dear Julius,

Flying to Senegal in one hour's time. What can I usefully say?

Yes, I agree with you that we are not seeing 'creeping nationalization' in Bakumba. The country is a mixed economy, and it will keep its dynamic private sector. The Government will not intervene much more than at present, i.e. in the oil industry, and a direct interest in banks, insurance, plus some commercial and industrial enterprises, such as the car industry.

One advantage for Blik is that the Government is anxious to maintain an effective level of employment. So it might not be willing to have a showdown with a company which is such a good provider of employment. On the other hand, the powerful religious and tribal groups make the country inherently unstable politically speaking.

What is indigenization leading to in Bakumba? In my view, the formation of a very strong, politically powerful and extremely wealthy new middle class, closely linked with traditional ruling classes of the country.

Finally, my dear Julius, I can offer no judgement on the long-term results of indigenization policies such as Bakumba's except that they are within the historical logic of transferring power from former colonial powers to the newly emerging states in Africa.

Haven't been much help, have I?

Regards,
Hanna

INSTRUCTIONS

Divide into two groups for preliminary discussion of the problem. One group will be composed of members of the Bakumban Department of Industry; the other will represent members of the Blik negotiating team.

The Bakumban group, led by the Minister of Industry, should consider what the Government will do if Blik:

(i) pull out of the country

(ii) give way completely

(iii) decide to negotiate for concessions.

The Blik team, led by the Corporation's Executive Vice-President, should decide what approach it will take in its negotiations with the Bakumban Department of Industry's officials.

Finally, the two groups should confront each other at the conference table and hammer out a compromise agreement about the future of Blik (Bakumba).

A TRAVELLING MAN

Steven van Dam claims never to have done a day's work in his life. In fact, he works extremely hard, running a one-man business which takes him regularly around Europe and Southeast Asia. He deals mainly in small consignments of luxury goods, but he will buy almost anything which he knows he can transport and sell without too much trouble and at a modest profit. He had his first business success at eighteen and was convinced he would be a millionaire at thirty. Today, at twenty-four, his bank balance is in credit and he is living the kind of life he enjoys; but commercial success seems somehow to elude him.

THE RIGHT PEOPLE

Steven depends entirely on personal contacts for his livelihood, and one contact above all: Usman Sanusi, businessman, of Surabaya. Most of the other people Steven does business with he meets through Sanusi's introduction, and most of what he knows about the formalities of foreign trade he has learnt from the older man.

Sanusi was once a close friend of Steven's father, and for a while, in the 1950s, they were in business together in Surabaya. Then van Dam Senior returned to Europe, after helping Sanusi to set up on his own as proprietor of a small garage. Sanusi had to struggle for years, overcoming all kinds of setbacks, before the economic climate changed. When it did change, however, he was well placed to take advantage of it, and by the late '70s was a wealthy man with business interests in several countries.

In 1975, van Dam was killed in a flying accident, and Sanusi, very upset by his old friend's death, wrote a letter to young Steven, whom he had never met. As a result, when Steven left school later the same year he flew to Jakarta and spent several weeks as the guest of Sanusi and his family. On his last day there he bought 500 of the cheap water-colour paintings that street vendors sell in the big cities. He took them to London, where he sold them as one lot to a retailer for a thousand pounds. His profit paid for his next flight to the East. Suddenly, he felt he knew what business was all about.

CUTTING THE APRON STRINGS

Steven has just returned to his flat in Amsterdam after the latest of many trips. It was an unusual one, and he is still not at all sure what to make of it, except that it will be a turning-point of some sort in his life.

In Surabaya, Usman Sanusi told him bluntly: 'It's time you stopped fooling about and went into business seriously. You can't go on peddling knick-knacks for ever, relying on my goodwill and my contacts! Your father helped me to get started, and I've tried to do the same for you. But now you've got to think for yourself, plan your career a little. Cigarette?'

Steven, taken aback by Sanusi's unexpected severity, lit a cigarette and recognized at once the sweet, pungent taste of cloves, mingled with fine Javanese tobacco.

'Ah . . . kretek!' he said. 'These are exceptionally good ones, too. No wonder my Indonesian friends in London are always asking me to take a few packets back for them. I wonder . . .?'

FIGURING IT OUT

Without saying anything to Sanusi, Steven took a taxi next day to Malang, a town in the hills about 100 kilometres south of Surabaya. There he found the factory where 'Cockatoo' brand cigarettes are made, and introduced himself to the owner of the firm: an energetic widow, Mrs Subroto.

'I took over the factory when my husband died two years ago,' she told him. 'It's very interesting work, but I don't know if I can keep going. The profits on domestic cigarette sales are too small to finance the rebuilding and re-equipping that our factory desperately needs. If only we could find a good export market!'

Negotiations did not take very long. Steven returned to Surabaya the next day, having exchanged formal letters with Mrs Subroto's company fixing the date, quantity and price of his first order. Sanusi was impressed, but seemed a little uneasy.

'A hundred thousand cigarettes a month!' he said. 'Can you sell that many in London?'

'Easily,' Steven assured him. 'But I'm planning to do much better than that. These kretek cigarettes are going to establish a new trend in smoking habits. In six months, I'm going to increase the order to 500,000 a month. For 25,000 packets, at 20p gross profit in English money, that's £5,000 a month. You were quite right, Usman. It is time I started to take life a bit more seriously.'

ENCOUNTER AT HEATHROW

Steven flew from Jakarta direct to London, with a couple of hundred 'Cockatoo' *kretek* cigarettes in his hand luggage. He declared them to the customs official but, instead of being waved on as he always had been in the past, he was asked to break open one of the packets for further inspection. The official sniffed suspiciously and asked questions about the contents of the cigarettes. Steven had to follow the man into a small room where he and all his luggage were thoroughly searched, and he was questioned closely by a senior customs officer. After an hour's delay, he was finally allowed to take his cigarettes and leave.

LEGAL ADVICE

Once in central London, Steven discussed the incident with his friend Mr Ong, who runs a Malaysian-Chinese store in Soho.

'It's not really surprising,' Ong said cheerfully. 'Naturally, they thought that you might be bringing in drugs.'

'If I had a dollar for every time I've refused to carry drugs for someone, I'd be a rich man by now,' Steven said. 'But what I'm worried about is what happens when I apply for an import licence. I never dreamt there'd be any problems. Maybe I need some legal advice. Can I use your phone?'

Scriven, Dinwiddy & Turner
SOLICITORS

N. B. Turner
V. J. Day
D. Pettersen

99, VESTIGE LANE
LONDON EC1

S. van Dam Esq.

1034 Vermeerlaan

Bylmeer

Netherlands

17 August 1981
Ref VJD/sh/1341

Dear Mr van Dam

    Following your recent visit to this office, when we talked about the possibility of obtaining a licence to import and distribute cigarettes containing cloves or clove essence from Southeast Asia, we have considered the legal position, particularly as regards the Department of Trade and Industry and the Customs and Excise authorities.

    It appears that excise duty would be payable on these cigarettes at the normal rate. However, the D.T.I. regulations make it clear that you might encounter serious obstacles and delays in obtaining the requisite licence, as the cloves might be considered an unacceptable additive. The tobacco would therefore be regarded as impure or adulterated, and the provisions of the Customs and Excise Act 1952 (as amended) would apply.

    I am afraid I cannot be very encouraging. I know your determination to import these cigarettes, however, and would suggest that you apply for a licence in the usual way. If, as seems likely, your application is refused, you could then consider making legal representations to the D.T.I. You would probably be called on to show that the substances mixed with the tobacco are not harmful or obnoxious in any way; you may wish to consider at this stage whether you would be able to furnish such evidence.

    My firm will of course be glad to advise you or to act for you at any time, and we shall await your further instructions.

Yours sincerely,

V. J. Day

THE OPTIONS

As a result of this letter, Steven spends a few days making further enquiries and finally decides he has the following options:

1 He can apply for a licence to mix tobacco and cloves and import the mixture in cigarettes. If his application is successful, he will get the licence in about six months. Although Mr Day is not optimistic, another lawyer thinks Steven has a 70 per cent chance of success.

In the meantime, the first six monthly consignments of *kretek* cigarettes will be shipped from Malang between January and July. The cigarettes will have to be stored at the port of entry pending the granting of the licence, or worse, the results of an appeal against the refusal of the application. In either case, storage costs could be high.

2 He can explain his problem to Mrs Subroto and ask to be released from the contract. He could reasonably be expected to pay a proportion of the ex-works price (up to about £700 for each month's consignment) by way of compensation. Mrs Subroto is not likely to sue him for breach of contract, or to win if she did.

3 He can anticipate opposition to *kretek* cigarettes (either from the authorities or from the anti-smoking lobby) by commissioning an analyst's report from a private consultant. This would take at least three months and cost a minimum of £1,000, but it would certainly lend strong support to his DTI application.

4 He can bring forward his more ambitious plans – in other words, 'think big' right from the start. Bigger orders would, if properly handled, lead to bigger profits. It would then be worthwhile for Steven to fight hard to get his import licence – even if it meant spending a lot of money on lawyers' and consultants' fees. If he finally failed to obtain the licence, however, he would be in very serious trouble indeed – probably bankrupt.

5 To strengthen his position, especially if he decides to aim for larger profits, he can propose that he and Usman Sanusi go into partnership. Sanusi has capital, friends, expertise; Steven has youth on his side and a good knowledge of European languages and markets. Together, they could achieve much.

NOTE

Steven's bank balance stands currently at about £800 in London, and the equivalent of about £2,500 in Amsterdam. He has personal assets valued at about £8,000.

INSTRUCTIONS

In small groups, consider the ways that are open to Steven and assess their advantages and disadvantages.

Then, meeting in one large group, decide what he should do, adding any provisos or conditions that you think may be necessary.

CARBONIDE:
Angry residents speak out

by Herald correspondent PETER GRIMBOLD

Residents of Newsea are to demand a government enquiry into pollution caused by the Carbonide works in their town. A public meeting in the Newsea Community Hall last night ended in uproar when bags of soot were hurled at Mr Lars Laurensen, the Norwegian manager of Carbonide in Newsea.

Earlier, the meeting heard Mrs Maggie Fulton, Chairman of the Residents' Action Committee, speak of the 'health hazard' and 'potential genetic threat' that hangs over Newsea in the shape of a heavy cloud of black smoke and powdery carbon dust. Local government representatives denied that fumes from the factory were toxic, but admitted that smoke was a nuisance and that heavy lorries approaching and leaving the factory were a danger to pedestrians. Two children have been killed in road accidents since Carbonide re-opened the former Newsea Town Mill as their factory in 1979, and there have been a number of injuries.

Mrs Fulton, a prospective Independent candidate at the next general election, pleaded at the start of the meeting for calm and rational debate of Newsea's problems. But her pleas were disregarded as housewives and wage-earners described the 'living hell' that had been forced on them by Carbonide's presence.

(Turn to back page, col. 6)

Mrs Fulton facing militant workers

BACKGROUND

The signboard outside the factory says: Newsea Chemicals (1979) Ltd. Underneath this name, much less conspicuous, is the parent company's logo: a circle, with the company's initials, ICC.

The International Carbonide Corporation is what the people of Newsea are fighting. It is not a large concern, as multinationals go, but it is highly capitalized and is believed to be making enormous profits.

Carbonide operates in highly sensitive areas. Its chemical products are vital to industry. Without them, many of the comforts of modern life, which we take for granted, would become unobtainable or very expensive. But the extraction and processing of these chemicals involve procedures that environmentalists often find unacceptable: open-cast mining, dumping of waste, pollution of the air and sea. Carbonide has therefore attracted a lot of unfavourable attention from responsible scientists as well as from politicians and ecologists. It has to work hard to convince its critics that society needs Carbonide, and that its policy is always to do the least possible damage to the natural surroundings.

Understandably, Carbonide prefers to keep a low profile. Its functions are decentralized, its subsidiaries are registered under unobtrusive names, and its senior executives are normally recruited from outside the regions in which they work. Newsea's manager, for instance, is a young Norwegian, Lars Laurensen.

Lars feels particularly concerned about the local residents' opposition, since his factory has created five hundred secure and well-paid jobs in this depressed area. He himself likes the town and has identified strongly with its citizens' efforts to revive its community life. Newsea grew up around the steel mill – built in the 1870s, uneconomic by the 1950s, closed in 1974. Without ICC, Newsea would probably have been a ghost town by now.

However, as Lars has often admitted to David Pugh, the local Medical Officer of Health, there is no getting away from the fact that carbon black is filthy stuff to work with, and this is what the factory mainly produces. It is a fine black powder, which is carried on every breeze and gets into everything. It is particularly unfortunate that the factory lies directly to windward of the residential part of the town, with the prevailing westerly winds blowing across it for at least two hundred and fifty days a year. The old steel mill was put there to be near the railway, but the branch line closed, the rails have been torn up, and access is now by narrow streets through which heavy lorries pass with difficulty.

These are local problems. National anger is much more likely to be aroused by reports in the press of a top secret project, known simply as Project 73, which is being carried out at Newsea. This is known to result in the emission of minute traces of lead compounds into the atmosphere. Could these accumulate and reach dangerous levels in the environment? The experts say no, but it will be years before anyone can really say for certain.

barnum upworth + clayman

public relations consultants   22a south edward street   london w2z 4yp

29 June 1982

Dear Lars

    Thank you for your letter and the newspaper cuttings. I was distressed to read of your difficulties at Newsea.

    Naturally we shall be glad to act on your firm's behalf, if instructed by you. I agree that there is no call for immediate action and, since you ask my advice, I must say that I think for Carbonide to react too strongly to recent events would only exacerbate public feeling. I am sure you are right to play it cool. As far as I can understand the situation at this distance, I believe there is every chance of a backlash developing among the employees of your company. Your own labour force are going to realize that five hundred jobs will be at stake if the residents get their government enquiry.

    The lorries are surely local government's worry, not yours. Presumably, the Borough Council saw the estimates of traffic density when Carbonide applied for permission to develop the site.

    Toxicity is clearly the major problem. No doubt your own analysts monitor factory wastes, air and water samples, etc. We would need to bring in some first-rate industrial chemists from the academic world if we wanted impartial evidence. However, it appears that only one or two of your processes produce any toxic materials, and then only in very small amounts. I would advise you not to say anything to the press about Project 73 that might be quoted, and don't talk to radio or TV interviewers for the time being. If they catch you outside your front door, the safest reply is always 'No comment'.

    Anyway, keep in touch and let me know if you would like me to come down to Newsea.

Yours,

Steven Barnum

Steven Barnum

Lars Laurensen Esq.
Newsea Chemicals Ltd
Newsea

POSSIBLE SOLUTIONS

Barnum's advice to 'play it cool' may be fine in the short term, but Laurensen knows he must decide quickly on a long-term policy for Newsea Chemicals. For one thing, there is now the real possibility of a public enquiry being made into the pollution allegedly caused by his factory. For another, there is a key job in Carbonide's Geneva office which will fall vacant next year.

Lars can see four possible courses of action.

1 He can call in Steven Barnum, whom he trusts implicitly, and put into his firm's expert hands the whole problem of Carbonide's image and Newsea Chemicals' relationship with the local residents. Barnum's fee is likely to be anything from £10,000 upwards, plus expenses. The cost of carrying out Barnum's recommendations could be far higher. He may suggest local TV/radio advertising; sponsoring of local sporting or cultural events; limiting the size or number of lorries coming to the factory, etc.

2 He can try to beat the opposition at their own game, by vigorously defending the firm's pollution record, using statistics to make the Residents' Action Committee look foolish or ill-informed, and reminding local people that Newsea Chemicals employs over 20 per cent of the town's workforce in an area of high unemployment. As long as he plays his cards right, the trade unions concerned will certainly back him. In money terms, this course of action will cost very little, but if it fails, the consequences will be disastrous.

3 He can give way gracefully to demands that Carbonide should 'clean up' the Newsea factory. Rebuilding the two chimneys and installing the most sophisticated filtering and air-cleansing equipment will cost about £1.5m. Screening the Project 73 work in concrete, and storing all wastes in steel cylinders buried on the premises, will cost £500,000 now and about £200,000 a year in running costs. In other words, profits will drop to zero for twelve to eighteen months, and will recover slowly thereafter.

4 It is quite out of the question to move the whole plant to another site. But he could, with as much fuss and fanfare as possible, get Project 73 moved elsewhere, perhaps to another country. This would not be difficult; Bangladesh, Guyana, Italy and Canada all have Carbonide subsidiaries that would jump at the chance to control this potential major growth area. Fewer than fifty jobs would be lost at Newsea, and fees for the transfer of patent rights would add substantially to his firm's – Newsea's – profits and reserves. Fleet Street would be appeased. But the locals would still have to live with carbon black and a growing number of heavy lorries.

INSTRUCTIONS

Divide into two groups, residents and factory management. Discuss the problem itself, and possible solutions, from the points of view of the following: the local residents; the trade union chiefly represented at the factory; Carbonide's head office; a Carbonide subsidiary in each group member's own country.

Then, each group should prepare its own strategy before meeting in one large group to decide what action Laurensen should take to safeguard Carbonide's interests in Newsea.

THE PROBLEM WITH ORANGES

Most people like oranges, but that does not necessarily mean they are easy to sell. If you start growing them for profit, you will soon discover that the major citrus-fruit markets of the world are shared among a handful of large, highly organized and very competitive producers or groups of producers working through state marketing boards. Breaking into these markets is a tough problem. Your oranges may be very good ones, but there is not much you can do to make them especially eye-catching or different from the competition. Your major difficulty will be to get your particular brand of oranges known and accepted by distributors in the trade and by consumers when both these groups are firmly attached to the brands of your competitors.

HOW AFJUZ BEGAN

A few years ago, the orange growers of a certain area of North Africa got together to set up, with the help of their government and Ministry of Agriculture, a Citrus Fruit Marketing Board. Thanks to a well-planned programme of research, irrigation, controlled breeding and soil enrichment, production of oranges has greatly increased and quality is now first-class. The Marketing Board's aim is to sell these luscious oranges overseas in large quantities, under the brand name of AFJUZ.

BRITAIN SELECTED AS FIRST OVERSEAS MARKET

An Egyptian marketing executive, Abdul Chamass, was appointed to develop overseas sales. He immediately contacted a marketing consultant from the United States, Helen Spandrel, who was based in London and had specialist knowledge of the citrus-fruit trade. She advised Chamass to concentrate on one country first, and suggested Britain as the first target. Chamass followed her advice, and on her recommendation gave the agency for AFJUZ oranges to Clutton and Cummings Ltd whose head office is in London.

A BAD START

The agent has now been operating for two and a half years, but sales have been very disappointing. Competing with established brands, AFJUZ has obtained a market share of only 0.8 per cent. This represents less than £½million worth of sales per annum while total sales of oranges in Britain amount to about £50 million.

The results are especially depressing because:

(i) Helen Spandrel had confidently predicted a market share of 3 per cent or more within three years

(ii) total imports of oranges into Britain have risen steadily during the last five years

(iii) AFJUZ oranges look and taste as good as those of competitors; also, they are from 2 to 3 per cent cheaper than other brands.

ACTION

Determined to work out a more effective sales strategy, Abdul Chamass and his assistant, Gamal El-Din, went on a tour of Britain. They talked to wholesalers, retailers, supermarket bosses, housewives, advertisers, greengrocers, hoteliers, and of course their agents, Clutton and Cummings. On returning to London, they arranged to meet Helen Spandrel to discuss their problems.

STRATEGIES

Helen Well, everyone who tries AFJUZ oranges likes them. Our tests have proved that.

Abdul Oh, the product's all right, and we have a record crop coming this season, but half of it will rot on the trees and some growers will go bankrupt if we can't sell it.

Gamal We could just cut the price in half. It's better to sell below cost than let them rot. If we can undercut all the others by a big enough margin, we're bound to get rid of that crop.

Helen That's called dumping, and it's no way to solve your problem. You're in trouble now because Clutton and Cummings haven't really reached the housewife. They . . .

Abdul They've concentrated too much on wholesalers who resell to the catering trade — restaurants, hotels and so on. That marketing channel accounts for only a small proportion of the total market.

Helen You mustn't expect miracles. The agent's had rather a limited advertising budget.

Gamal I couldn't agree more. We've been too tight-fisted, in my view.

Abdul Well, Gamal, someone at Head Office seems to have heard about your views. I received a telex this morning informing me that the UK budget is to be doubled for the next two years. It's been put up to £100,000 instead of the usual £50,000. Mind you, they expect us to get three per cent of the market — that's a minimum target. There's no reason why we shouldn't do it. It's simply a question of choosing the right marketing strategy. I've got some proposals here.

FOUR PROPOSALS

Here are the proposals Abdul Chamass presented for discussion at the meeting.

1 John Smith and Co., Fruit and Vegetable Importers

Smith's have depots at all the major fruit markets throughout Britain. They propose that AFJUZ oranges should be promoted to independent specialist greengrocers. These small shops handle perhaps 60 per cent of all citrus fruit sold in Britain, and Smith's claim to have a good relationship or contacts with as many as half of them. They recommend that part of the £100,000 budget should be spent on display material such as posters, banners, wall charts, plastic shopping bags and eye-catching mobiles, etc. These would be distributed to shopkeepers through wholesalers. The remainder of the budget could be used for advertising in trade journals. Smith's are willing to place an immediate order for £30,000 worth of oranges if their ideas are accepted. Further orders would depend on sales.

2 Dunne Bros, Imported Fruit Wholesalers

This small but expanding firm, based in Newcastle, operates in Northeast England and southern Scotland. They have offered to organize a regional promotion in their area. They claim that for £100,000 they could make a big impact by using regional media. The region in fact only accounts for 18 per cent of the total national market, but a good share of this regional market could represent a big improvement on AFJUZ's present performance. The one-month promotion campaign they propose would include advertising on local TV, radio, and in local newspapers, together with posters for shops. The campaign would also include use of a hot-air balloon with an AFJUZ tail-streamer. This would carry merchandisers dressed in AFJUZ tee-shirts. They would alight at towns in the region distributing prizes and promotional literature. In return for using their sales force in the campaign, Dunne Bros have asked for exclusive rights to distribute AFJUZ in their region. They will also put the Marketing Board in touch with similar firms in other areas if this scheme is successful.

3 Vasco Supermarkets Ltd

This group's chief purchasing executive has offered to stock and display AFJUZ oranges in all the company's 500 stores. He mentions that Vasco's account for over 8 per cent of orange sales in Britain. They are prepared to feature AFJUZ for four weeks in the weekly full-page newspaper advertisements which appear throughout the country announcing the special prices and new products which are being offered by their stores. Vasco's would expect the Marketing Board to pay £100,000 towards the cost of these advertisements. As a gesture of good faith, the company will place an immediate order for £60,000 worth of stock. Further orders will depend on the public's response to the oranges. Vasco asks for exclusive rights to handle AFJUZ in Britain, but will continue to offer all brands of citrus fruit for sale in their stores.

4 Clutton and Cummings, Agents

Clutton's have frequently complained about the small advertising budget. When told it was to be doubled, they asked Abdul Chamass to 'give them another chance as agent'. They have proposed that the £100,000 should not be used on promotion at all. Instead, the money should be spent on offering new customers in the trade a special discount of 10 per cent. A price reduction of this size would obviously attract supermarket buyers, wholesalers and importers. Once housewives had tried AFJUZ oranges, they would be willing to buy this brand again, and it would then become well established. After the money had been used up on this subsidy, the discount could be discreetly withdrawn, but customers would be 'hooked' on AFJUZ.

INSTRUCTIONS

Students should first divide into small groups for preparatory discussion of the problem. They might like to approach the case by considering these two questions:

(i) What are the advantages and disadvantages of the proposals which have been made?

(ii) Should one of the proposals be recommended to the Board? Or should a totally new approach be adopted?

The groups should then come together under the leadership of a chairman to try to reach a decision concerning the future development of AFJUZ sales in Britain.

KYOSEC

MINIATURE COLOUR TV MIRACLE!!

TECHNICAL SPECIFICA

— standard colour
stereo radio cassette
order

Screen size:	10cm
Receiving Channel:	CCIR VHF UHF

Automatic fine-tuning

Radio Bands:	SW MW FM

Audio output:	3W
Power input rating:	A 5

Power consumption:

Transistors:

Diodes:

ICs:

Dimensions:

Weight:

if INDUSTRIAS FUTURAS S.A.
1000 Av. Einstein · São Paolo · Brasil

Mr Nam—Hoon Chun
Kyoung—Sung Electrical Co. Ltd
Masan
South Korea

15 September 1981

Dear Mr Chun

We confirm our telex of today's date and enclose
our order no. 27901 for 150 Kyosec colour-
cassette TV sets, model CVC 90.

Early delivery of these sets is most earnestly
requested, in view of the very favourable
customer response to our demonstration models.
We confidently expect demand to build up rapidly,
and on behalf of retailers would welcome your
assurance that you will continue to supply large-
scale orders with your usual promptness.

My colleague Mrs Noya sends her respects and
looks forward to meeting you in Masan next
month.

Yours sincerely

Arturo Bello

General Manager
Industrias Futuras S.A.

THE FIRM

Kyoung-Sung Electrical Co. Ltd is a large, aggressive manufacturing company, located in the city of Masan in South Korea. It is less than ten years old but it is highly profitable and it has an enviable reputation for the quality and reliability of its products. It makes radios, hi-fi systems, TVs and TV games, and various control and computing devices for the home. Some of its product lines are exported under the brand name Kyosec, mainly to South America.

The company is financed partly by private investors (many of them overseas), partly by the South Korean Government, and partly by a group of Australian banks. These banks operate through an Australian-registered company, Brismel Investments, and about a dozen senior Kyoung-Sung managers in the financial and marketing divisions are Brismel appointees.

Profits last year were US$8.5m, and are expected to top US$10m this year.

THE PRODUCTS

There are three Kyosec products that concern us. All of them are tape recorders which record television pictures on magnetic tape contained in a cassette. These machines use two types of cassette:

B. compact cassette (smaller than a post card; until recently, used only for sound recording)

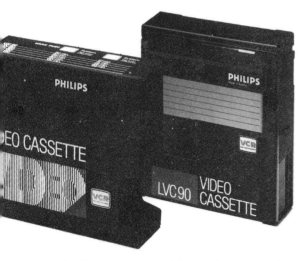

A. standard TV cassette (about the same size and weight as a book)

A year ago, Kyoung-Sung designers were looking for a way to record black and white TV pictures and mono sound together on a compact (type B) cassette. Several other manufacturers were racing towards the same goal. Then the impossible happened. A young engineer stumbled on a technique for recording *colour* TV and *stereo* sound simultaneously on the magnetic tape (only 4mm wide) of a compact cassette. Kyoung-Sung leapfrogged over the heads of their rivals.

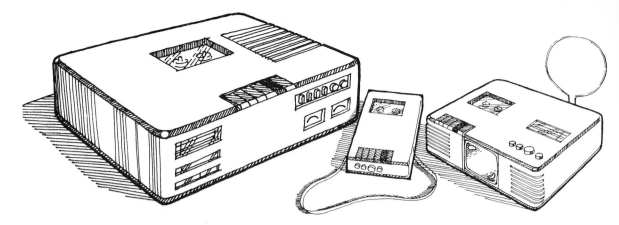

These are the three tape recorders.

1 The VC 11 video cassette recorder (VCR). Launched about a year ago; selling well in major Kyosec markets. Uses standard TV cassettes; compatible with almost any modern television receiver. The size of a small suitcase and weighs about twelve kilos.

2 The Starstripe 100 miniature VCR. Still in the development and proving stage. Will record up to two hours of colour TV on a compact cassette, and will be compatible with any TV receiver. It is this requirement of compatibility which is creating technical problems at the moment. Probably won't be on the market for another nine to twelve months.

3 The CVC 90 stereo radio cassette recorder, with 10cm colour TV and full colour TV recording on compact cassette. The technical problems of the Starstripe don't arise here because the CVC 90 is not used with other TV equipment. Kyosec therefore plan to go into full production of the CVC 90 almost at once. Considerably smaller than the VC 11: the size of a small briefcase and weighs about five kilos.

THE PROBLEM

It is, unfortunately, at the production stage that Kyoung-Sung is most vulnerable. Every available square metre of factory floor space is devoted to making and assembling the complex stages of the receiver and recorder. Production of standard components is, as far as possible, subcontracted to other firms. The biggest subcontract is with the Dong-A Company, who manufacture the 10cm picture tubes. There is nothing remarkable about these tubes, except that they are unusually small for a colour set. Dong-A have just delivered the first month's order of 10,000 tubes, and have another 5,000 on the road, when disaster strikes. The Dong-A factory is burned to the ground. The company, which had not been too healthy before it won the Kyoung-Sung contract, goes into liquidation. So who will make colour picture tubes for Kyoung-Sung's miracle baby now?

FINDING A SUPPLIER

Urgent enquiries are telexed to every likely source of TV components.

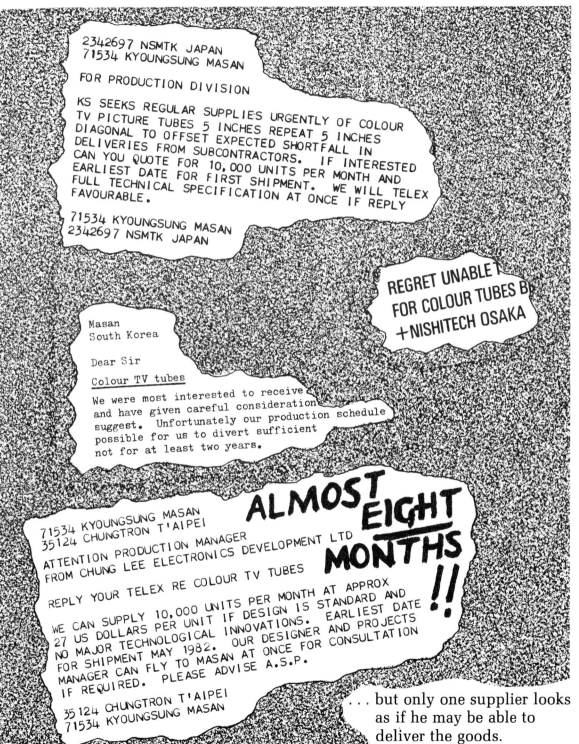

... but only one supplier looks as if he may be able to deliver the goods.

POSSIBLE STRATEGIES

WE'VE GOT SIX WEEKS' STOCK OF COLOUR TUBES IN HAND. WE CAN LAUNCH THE NEW SET, GO INTO PRODUCTION AND KEEP OUR FINGERS CROSSED THAT WE FIND A SUPPLIER BEFORE THE BACKLOG'S EXHAUSTED.

OF COURSE, YOU COULD DELAY YOUR LAUNCH DATE UNTIL YOUR SUPPLIES OF COLOUR TUBES FROM TAIWAN ARE ASSURED: BUT THAT WOULD MEAN LOSING SIX TO EIGHT MONTHS. YOUR LEAD OVER YOUR COMPETITORS COULD BE WIPED OUT.

THERE'S A THIRD POSSIBILITY - USE BLACK AND WHITE TUBES! WE CAN GET THOSE ANYWHERE - SIMPLIFY THE CIRCUIT DESIGN, CUT THE PRICE AND STILL BE ONE JUMP AHEAD OF THE REST!

MY SUGGESTION WOULD BE TO BRING FORWARD YOUR MINIATURIZED VCR DECK FOR USE WITH STANDARD TV COLOUR RECEIVERS.* I KNOW THE DESIGNERS WANT MORE TIME, BUT YOU'RE GOING TO HAVE TO GAMBLE ON SOMETHING.

THE STARSTRIPE 100

MR NAM-HOON CHUN
VICE-PRESIDENT IN
CHARGE OF OPERATIONS,
KYOUNG-SUNG ELECTRICAL
SOUTH KOREA

MRS LUISA NOYA
HEAD OF MARKETING,
INDUSTRIAS FUTURAS S.A.
SAO PAULO, BRAZIL

MR ALEC STANSFIELD
OVERSEAS INVESTMENT
DIRECTOR,
BRISMEL INVESTMENTS
PTY AUSTRALIA

MR ROBERT LEE
ASSISTANT BRAND
MANAGER FOR
KYOSEC PRODUCTS,
KYOUNG-SUNG ELECTRICAL

The market for electronic consumer goods is worldwide, but savagely competitive. The options for Kyoung-Sung all look pretty unpleasant, but they must choose one of them – unless someone can come up with a new alternative.

INSTRUCTIONS

First, meet in four small groups. Each group should consider the advantages and disadvantages of one of the options. Work out what its implications are likely to be, for Kyoung-Sung and for its distributors. Invent any small details that are needed to complete your discussion.

Then, meeting in one large group, decide what you would advise Kyoung-Sung to do. The chairman of the group may like to guide the discussion along these lines:

(i) Remind the group of the major factors in the problem.

(ii) Assess the importance to Kyoung-Sung of the CVC 90. What does the company stand to gain or to lose by launching its new product now – or later?

(iii) Consider the options one by one, and compare them with each other and any new ideas that the group may have thought of. How would each course of action affect the company's policy, sales and development?

(iv) Decide which option to recommend – adding provisos or conditions if you wish.